Women and Islam

Women and Islam

Myths, Apologies, and the Limits of Feminist Critique

Ibtissam Bouachrine

LEXINGTON BOOKS
Lanham • Boulder • New York • Toronto • Plymouth, UK

Published by Lexington Books
A wholly owned subsidary of Rowman & Littlefield
4501 Forbes Boulevard, Suite 200, Lanham, Maryland 20706
www.rowman.com

10 Thornbury Road, Plymouth PL6 7PP, United Kingdom

British Library Cataloguing in Publication Information Available

Library of Congress Cataloging-in-Publication Data

Bouachrine, Ibtissam.
Women and Islam : myths, apologies, and the limits of feminist critique / Ibtissam Bouachrine.
p. cm.
Includes bibliographical references and index.
ISBN 978-0-7391-7906-2 (cloth) — ISBN 978-0-7391-7907-9 (electronic)
ISBN 978-0-7391-9405-8 (pbk : alk paper)
1. Women in Islam. 2. Feminism—Religious aspects—Islam. I. Title.
BP173.4.B68 2014
297.082—dc23
2014010403

Printed in the United States of America

For Hayate al-Noufous El-Hajjali and Bouchaib Bouachrine

Contents

Acknowledgments

This book owes much to the rich intellectual community at Smith College. I owe particular debts of gratitude to Kenneth Stow for his support of my work and for his critical guidance. Many thanks to the entire Spanish and Portuguese Department and Middle East Studies Program especially Estela Harretche, Marguerite Harrison, Reyes Lázaro who have been sources of inspiration. This book could not have been written without the generous mentoring of the strong feminists at Smith, Donna Divine and Pamela Petro, to name a few.

I am also profoundly grateful to the many mentors I have had throughout my life. At West Virginia University, Judith Gold Stitzel and Kathleen McNerney introduced me to the study of women and gender. At Florida State University, Santa Arias challenged me to explore premodern history with a feminist eye. At Tulane University, Jean Dangler inspired my career.

I have often relied on the support of good friends in times of self-doubt. I thank them for their valuable insight, encouragement, and friendship: Yoel Ohayon, Idelber Avelar, and Rabbi Justin David. Douglas Lane Patey and Anouar Majid encouraged me to think critically beyond the sacred. My office neighbor Payal Banerjee reminded me that laughter, pleasure, and feminism go together. I am equally indebted to the audiences at the universities where I was invited to share my ideas early on: University of Massachusetts in Amherst, Harvard University, the Catalan Center at New York University, and Institut National des Langues et Civilisations Orientales. I thank Claire Huttlinger for her keen editorial eye and for her rigorous standards. I also thank the editors at Lexington Books, especially Sarah Ghulamali, Justin Race and Brian Hill for believing in this book from the beginning and for supporting me at every stage of this project.

Beyond these debts, I wish to thank all my students at Smith College. Thank you for indulging me while I made the case for Lil' Wayne in the study of the Mediterranean. Special thanks to Elizabeth (Bethy) Williams, who was invaluable as my research assistant during a crucial stage of the project.

An earlier version of a portion of Chapter 1 appeared as "In the Absence of Men: Representing Andalusi Women's Sexuality in the Context of Military Conflict," *Journal of Medieval Iberia* 4, 1 (2012) (www.tandfonline.com); an earlier version of a portion of Chapter 5 appeared in French as "*Rjal* et leurs reines: Le printemps arabe et le discours sur la masculinité et la féminité," *NAQD: Revue d'Etudes et de Critique Sociale* 29 (2012); an earlier version of a portion of Chapter 2 appeared as "Zoraida, the Other Author of the Quixote," Al-Masar Journal 13 (2012). All are reproduced with permission of the editors and publishers. The completion of this study was facilitated by generous grants from the Provost's Office at Smith College and a summer seminar grant from the National Endowment for the Humanities. For this support, I am truly thankful.

Last, but not least, I thank my brother, Tachfine Bouachrine, for his love, encouragement, and belief in this project, and my sister, Hind Bouachrine, who has influenced this book right from its inception and read it in its numerous incarnations. Finally, I owe my greatest debt to my parents, Hayat al-Noufous El-Hajjali and Bouchaib Bouachrine, who made great sacrifices to educate me even when they were advised against investing so much in a woman's intellect. It is to them that I dedicate this book, with love, admiration, and gratitude.

Introduction

On Saturday, March 10, 2012, sixteen-year-old Amina Filali killed herself after she was severely beaten by her husband, who had also raped her. Under Article 475 of the Moroccan penal code, a rapist is allowed to marry his victim in order to avoid prosecution. Fearing public humiliation and the stigma of no longer being a virgin, Filali was forced to marry the man who had raped her at age fifteen, and who continued to abuse her physically throughout their marriage. When she realized that neither the law nor society could be invoked to rescue her, she committed suicide by swallowing rat poison.[1]

On Saturday, March 17, 2012, thirty-three-year-old Fakhra Younus jumped from a sixth-floor window in Rome, Italy. Twelve years earlier, her ex-husband, a Pakistani man from a wealthy and prominent family, had attacked her with acid. She underwent thirty-nine separate surgeries to reconstruct her face and body. When she could no longer bear the pain and injustice, she too killed herself.[2]

In July 2012, a twenty-two-year-old Afghani woman identified as Najibia was executed in Parwan Province in front of a cheering crowd. The brutal event was captured in an amateur three-minute video. Her alleged crime was adultery.[3]

Though they may appear to be extreme, these are not isolated stories. Muslim women of all ages, economic status, educational backgrounds, sexual orientations, and from different parts of historically Muslim countries, suffer the kinds of atrocities that not only violate common understandings of human rights and normally denounced as criminal or pathological and yet are sustained because they uphold some religious doctrine or some custom blessed by local traditions. Ironically, while instances of abuse meted out to women and even female children are routine, scholarship about Muslim women in the post 9/11 era has rarely focused attention on them preferring to speak of women's agency and resistance. Too few scholars are willing to tell the actual complicated and at times harrowing stories of Muslim women's lives. *Women and Islam: Myths, Apologies, and the Limits of Feminist Critique* radically rethinks the celebratory discourse constructed around Muslim women's resistance. It shows instead the limits of such resistance and the restricted agency given women within Islamic societies. The first chapters concentrate on premodern sources, although the book as a whole does not center on a single historical period. Rather, it is organized as a response to five questions that have been central to upholding the 'resistance discourse': What is the impact of the myth of al-Andalus on a feminist critique? What is the feminist utility of Edward Said's theory of Orientalism? Is Islam compatible with a feminist agenda? To what extent can Islamic institutions, such as the veil, be liberating for women? Will the current Arab uprisings yield significant change for Muslim women?

Women have long been a central symbol of the Muslim world, for those both within and without Islam's religious borders. Unsurprisingly, in the decade since 9/11, debates about Muslim women have attracted still greater interest, opening up the study of Islam and Muslim societies to new and varied perspectives. Prior to 2001, the study of both had been mostly ghettoized by language, historical period, geographic area, religion, or academic discipline. In response to the notion that women are oppressed under Islam, prominent feminists such as Miriam Cooke, Saba Mahmood, Amina Wadud, Margot Badran, and Leila Ahmed have uncovered what they labeled a feminist consciousness grounded in Islam.[4] Their work rethinks what traditionally have been interpreted as sites of injustice and oppression, such as religious ritual and theology or institutions such as the veil, as strategies for resisting patriarchy, and for asserting identity and expressing political engagement.

Other scholars, such as Lila Abu-Lughod, have interpreted the West's concern with Muslim women as one more extension of a colonialist feminism and imperialism, which pose as "saviors" of the subaltern women, but are really justifications for tightening Western political and economic controls on these societies.[5] Meanwhile, when criticisms of the inferior status of Muslim women are offered by scholars such as Marnia Lazreg, Ibn Warraq, and Salman Rushdie, who were born and lived in the Muslim world and therefore have an inside knowledge of its societies and cultures, such writers are dismissed as being "Western apologists" and "native informants" who fuel Islamophobia and opportunistically employ the political conflicts between the West and Islam for their own personal gain.[6]

It goes without saying that religion is not solely responsible for the oppression of all Muslim women. Nevertheless, silencing the critique of Islamic societies out of fear of assisting imperialism or promoting a negative image of Islam has led some feminist scholars to what Lebanese intellectual Mai Ghoussoub calls an "accommodation of obscurantism."[7] Using Muslim women and a defense of Islam as an oblique way to criticize the West cannot benefit women. Moreover, even though the rhetoric of the subordinate's resistance does appeal to scholars and their audiences, the academically fashionable insistence upon Muslim women's resistance can bolster systems of inequality and dominance that are at the root of oppression experienced by women. As feminist philosopher Susan Bordo has argued, the exaggerated use of the rhetoric of resistance can come to benefit oppressors, as "objectively [. . .] constraining, enslaving, and even murderous" conditions are reinterpreted as "liberating, transforming and life giving."[8]

In *Women and Islam,* I adopt an unapologetic and committed feminist critique of Islamic societies, one that dares to cross the boundaries of the sacred and does not hide behind veils of political correctness or cultural relativism. As Iranian feminist Haideh Moghissi puts it, "The best way to express solidarity with the Muslim diaspora is not to keep silent about oppressive features of one's own cultural tradition or the inhumane practices of fundamentalist regimes." Nor should one participate "in the destructive defensiveness which has shaped anti-colonial imagination in Islamic societies—to refuse self-glorification and self-pity."[9] Thus, this book calls for a shift away from the unproductive paradigm of "us" vs. the West, and it both challenges and calls for further challenge to the long celebrated myths and ideologies that have circulated in academic, as well as non-academic circles, whether within or outside the Muslim world.

Even though the "West" is a geographically defined territory that includes parts of the Muslim world nor is Islam limited to any particular region or continent, this book retains these terms as analytical tools. This is not to suggest that either the West or Islam is monolithic. Indeed, by crossing historical, linguistic, and disciplinary boundaries, this study seeks to highlight the heterogeneity of both Western and Islamic discourses about Muslim women. I also intend to demonstrate the variety of women's representations and experiences in the western Mediterranean, a region that has previously been neglected in the scholarship about Islam. Although recent years have seen numerous publications about Muslim women, most of these focus on parts of the Muslim world, such as the Middle East and the Indian subcontinent, perhaps because of their political relevance to the West.

This book is divided into five chapters. The first, "Dangerous Myths: Muslim Women *Before* the Age of Orthodoxy," questions the accuracy of widely held assumptions about al-Andalus, or Muslim Iberia from 711 to 1492, as a "Golden Age" for women under Islam and the feminist utility of such assumptions. Moreover, by historicizing the abundant treatises of sex and love from al-Andalus and North Africa, this chapter seeks to problematize the construction of the Islamic past as a time before orthodoxy. It exposes how falsehoods about the status of Andalusi women are used today in Islamic societies in order to silence critique and prevent true reform.

Chapter 2, "Sex in Context: Western Representations and the Limits of Edward Said's *Orientalism*," challenges assertions about French and Iberian representations of Muslim women. Said's influential work *Orientalism* has had an enduring impact on the study of Muslim women in Western literature and art. This chapter introduces a large corpus of premodern texts that suggest more nuance in the West's understanding of Islam and Muslims than Said and his followers are willing to acknowledge. This chapter is also critical of Saidians' dangerous protectionist discourse about Muslim culture, which seeks to confine Muslim women within identities imagined in opposition to the West.

Chapter 3, "Sacred Limits: Islamic Feminism, or Feminism Confined" shifts to Islamic feminists who, like Saidians and the proponents of the myth of al-Andalus, imagine that there is an "authentic" Islamic culture defined in opposition to Western values. Focusing on the work of the prominent Moroccan feminist Fatima Mernissi, this chapter describes the strategies used by Islamic feminists to argue for the compatibility of Islamic practices and feminism, and how such supposed compatibility has even infiltrated U.S. foreign policy discourse about Muslim women and Muslim societies. This compatibility, however, is fragile and is constantly put to the test when confronted with the inflexible boundaries of the sacred. As one example of this incompatibility, chapter 4, "Veiled Apologies: Muslim Women and The Truth about Choice," examines the myth of the veil's liberating function. This chapter explores how, in their defense of the veil, Western feminists such as Naomi Wolf construct an apologetic discourse that actually contradicts their earlier feminist commitments. Narratives from Muslim societies, on the other hand, reveal how patriarchal strategies coerce women into veiling.

The last chapter, "The Fallen Queens of Islam: How the Arab Revolutions Are Failing Women," looks toward the future, concentrating on the so-called Arab Spring. It is often assumed that democracy leads to promotion of women's rights. The uprisings in North Africa, however, reveal that as the fall of dictators has enabled previously marginalized Islamist parties to access political power, the new governments are far from establishing gender equality in Muslim societies. Indeed, these upheavals reveal just how deeply entrenched patriarchy is in the Muslim psyche.

Even though this study focuses on the representations and experiences of Muslim women within Muslim societies, it also has some practical ramifications for the West's relationship with predominantly Muslim countries. In today's interconnected world, the deaths of Amina Filali, Fakhra Younus, and Najibia are no longer just the responsibility of their respective countries. They are also the responsibility of the West and of all of those who are concerned with women's rights. In light of changing political conditions in North Africa and the Middle East, the United States and other Western governments can no longer afford to support a foreign policy that turns a blind eye to the injustice endured by half of these countries' populations. It is time for the U.S. to adopt a committed feminist foreign policy, one that will not attempt in relativist fashion to understand Amina Filali's death simply in the context of her culture's practices and beliefs. Like their counterparts in the West, Muslim women are deserving of life, liberty, and the pursuit of happiness.

NOTES

1. Hassan Hamdani, "Scandale: Amina, victime de la loi," *TelQuel*, 26 March 2012, available at http://www.telquel-online.com/Actualites/Maroc/scandale-amina-victime-de-la-loi/515 (25 May 2012).

2. See her obituary at http://www.telegraph.co.uk/news/obituaries/9207608/Fakhra-Younus.html (25 May 2012).

3. Christine Roberts, "Woman Executed by Taliban While Crowd Cheers," *New York Daily News*, 8 July 2012, available at http://articles.nydailynews.com/2012-07-08/news/32591738_1_afghan-woman-public-execution-taliban-commander (25 May 2012).

4. See Miriam Cooke, *Women Claim Islam: Creating Islamic Feminism Through Literature* (New York: Routledge, 2001), Saba Mahmood, *Politics of Piety: The Islamic Revival and the Feminist Subject* (Princeton: Princeton University Press, 2004), Amina Wadud, *Inside the Gender Jihad: Women's Reform in Islam* (Oxford: Oneworld, 2006), Margot Badran's *Feminism in Islam: Secular and Religious Convergences* (Oxford: Oneworld, 2009), and Leila Ahmed's *A Quiet Revolution: The Veil's Resurgence, from the Middle East to America* (New Haven: Yale University Press, 2011).

5. Lila Abu-Lughod, "Do Muslim Women Really Need Saving? Anthropological Reflections on Cultural Relativism and Its Others," *American Anthropologist* 104 (2002): 783–90.

6. See Adam Shatz, "The Native Informant," *The Nation*, 10 April 2003, available at http://www.thenation.com/article/native-informant?page=0,1 (25 May 2012). Hamid Dabashi dedicates an entire book to the critique of scholars such as Azar Nafisi, Fouad Ajami, and Ibn Warraq, whom he sees as the brown-skinned accomplices of the Bush administration between 2000 and 2008. See Hamid Dabashi, *Brown Skin, White Masks* (London: Pluto Press, 2011).

7. Mai Ghoussoub, "Feminist—or the Eternal Masculine—in the Arab World," *New Left Review* 161 (January-February 1987): 17.

8. Susan Bordo, *Unbearable Weight: Feminism, Western Culture, and the Body* (Berkeley: University of California Press, 1993), 168.

9. Haideh Moghissi, *Feminism and Islamic Fundamentalism: The Limits of Postmodern Analysis* (London: Zed Books, 1999), 4.

ONE

Dangerous Myths

Muslim Women Before *the Age of Orthodoxy*

The question of women in al-Andalus (Iberia under Muslim political control between 711 and 1492) continues to fascinate scholars and the general public alike. To borrow the words of the poet Victor Hernández Cruz, "The condition of women in al-Andalus was [. . .] much more advanced than in other parts of the world. Many women poets cultivated their poems, and both women and men touched upon erotic themes openly. No Islamic society has been this open ever since."[1] Indeed, what does one make of Muslim women from the eleventh, twelfth, and thirteenth centuries who demand to be satisfied sexually, invite their lovers into their beds, even instruct them about how to make love? And what about the many sexual treatises in which prominent religious scholars tell stories of sexually active, promiscuous, and unapologetic Muslim women who freely take on lovers, both male *and* female? This surely reflects a "Golden Age" for women under Islam, a time *before* orthodoxy, if one adheres to the general agreement among scholars, including Muslim feminists. This chapter examines the accuracy of such assumptions as well their implications for Muslim women. The first section argues that both Muslim and non-Muslim scholars are complicit in the construction of the myth of al-Andalus as the age before orthodoxy, seen as welcoming Muslim women's agency and empowerment. The second and third parts of the chapter historicize the literature produced by and about women in al-Andalus. They argue that, when read in their historical context, poems, love tales, and sexual treatises expose masculine anxiety about women's transgressive behavior, in particular a fear of women's sexual agency and the possible subversion of heterosexual norms. The final section looks at the "feminist utility" of al-Andalus as an "ennobling lie." It identifies five

1

reasons why the Andalusi myth is not productive and, from a feminist standpoint, can even be dangerous.

THE MYTH OF AL-ANDALUS, OR THE AGE BEFORE ORTHODOXY

In 1492, Spain coalesced as a nation-state, Columbus sailed to the Americas, and Jews were expelled from Iberia. In the wake of 9/11 that historical year acquired even greater significance, particularly regarding the relationship between Islam and the West. To scholars, fiction writers, and politicians alike, 1492 came to signify the *end* of a tolerant Islam that was able to flourish in Europe thanks to its tolerance of other religions and the *beginning* of an "extremist" and intolerant Islam whose violence culminated in the tragic events of 9/11. In *The Ornament of the World: How Muslims, Jews and Christians Created a Culture of Tolerance in Medieval Spain*, María Rosa Menocal writes that "after the events of September 11, which make us read and hear everything somewhat differently—most of all, of course, anything having to do with Islam and with its relationship to other religions and cultures—it seems impossible to understand the history of what was once, indeed, an ornament of the world without seeing reflections of that history right at our front door."[2] Similarly, Spanish novelist Juan Goytisolo, who is also greatly influenced by Américo Castro's concept of *convivencia* (living together) according to which medieval Iberia's different religious groups lived together peacefully, has constructed in his novels and political essays a romanticized and idealized Islamic medieval Iberia that stands in contrast to later orthodoxies.[3] Such celebration of al-Andalus as the age before Orthodoxy has even infiltrated the U.S. political discourse. In a speech he delivered at Cairo University on June 4, 2009, President Barack Obama referred to al-Andalus as a model of religious freedom that today's Muslim societies should follow: "Islam has a proud tradition of tolerance. We see it in the history of Andalusia and Cordoba during the Inquisition."[4] Thus, without truly investigating the multifaceted nature of this history, the myth of al-Andalus is being utilized to justify ideologies and political causes.

In spite of the efforts of scholars who have sought to dispel the myth of Iberia's *convivencia*, it continues to appeal to academics and non-academics alike.[5] On the one hand, the myth caters to a yearning for a successfully pluralistic and integrated society.[6] On the other hand, and more importantly, the idealization of al-Andalus creates a stage from which Islamic practices can be criticized safely without exposing one to the risk of being accused of "Islamophobia." It is often repeated by Muslims and non-Muslims alike that the "problem" today is "Islamic fundamentalists," *not* Islam itself.[7] The myth of al-Andalus confirms that indeed a tolerant Muslim society once did exist. In other words, Menocal, Goytisolo, and Obama are not critical of Islam itself, since they believe it capable of tolerance as its past demonstrates, but rather, they are critical of Muslims *today*. As Harold Bloom puts it in his forward to *The Ornament of the World*: "There are no Muslim Andalusians visible anywhere in the world today. The Iran of the ayatollahs and the Afghanistan of the Taliban may mark an extreme, but even Egypt is now not much of a culture of tolerance."[8] Therefore, while societies are usually valued for their "progress," the Muslims' burden is to *return* to their medieval "Golden Age."

The West is not solely to blame for the Andalusi myth. In postcolonial literature from the Muslim world, al-Andalus came to represent a utopia. Prominent Moroccan and Algerian novelists such as Tahar Benjelloun and Assia Djebar have mourned the loss of an idealized Andalus.[9] Ironically, even though anti-Semitism is increasing throughout the Muslim world, al-Andalus is more than ever celebrated as the "Golden Age" of a plural Muslim society.[10] For example, in Morocco high-budget international academic conferences, music festivals, and other cultural events are regularly organized around the themes of al-Andalus and Andalusi *convivencia* in order to construct the image internationally of a modern Muslim state tolerant of religious difference.

At the individual level, the myth of *convivencia* can serve as an answer to the existential dilemma that Muslims face today: What does it mean to be an ethical Muslim in the global world? Muslims are conflicted by the intersection of their Islamic beliefs and practices on the one hand, and what are perceived as Western values and principles, such as religious pluralism and the right to profess and practice the religion of one's choice, on the other. The myth of al-Andalus, however, places Islam above any ethical dilemma since tolerance and *convivencia* had already been accomplished in the past. It is therefore the Muslim's duty to achieve it again. Nevertheless, it is not a pressing matter since the "original" religious message is always already absolved.

When it comes to the highly controversial issue of women in Islam, al-Andalus has been constructed as the time before Islamic patriarchy in order to demonstrate "authentic" Islam's compatibility with women's emancipation. To Muslim feminists such as Moroccan intellectual Fatima Mernissi and Ugandan-born Canadian activist Irshad Manji, al-Andalus represents a time when Islam was accommodating of religious difference and respectful of women's rights. Historically influential women such as Subh, Wallada, and I'timad al-Rumaykiyah are often held up as examples of women's accomplishments in al-Andalus: skilled politicians and masterful poets, who embraced their femininity and publicly flaunted their sexuality. In response to Pakistani fundamentalists' objection to the appointment of Benazir Bhutto as the country's prime minister in 1988 on the grounds that it was religiously illegitimate, Mernissi dedicated her book *The Forgotten Queens of Islam* to recovering the memory of powerful Muslim women.[11] She evokes examples of premodern women including

Subh, who went from being a *jarya* (slave) to becoming *malikat Qurtuba* (queen of Cordoba), the favorite wife of the Umayyad Caliph al-Hakam II (r.961–76) and the mother of another Caliph, Hisham II (976–1009 and 1010–13). Citing Subh and other women from the Islamic past, Mernissi seeks to demonstrate that not only is it religiously acceptable for a woman to be involved in politics, but that, in fact, several women occupied the highest political position as heads of states.

Similarly, in her controversial book *The Trouble with Islam: A Muslim's Call for Reform in Her Faith*, Irshad Manji writes that "Islam was not always closed minded. During the 'Golden Age'—between the ninth and eleventh century—there existed a tradition of critical thinking in the Muslim world." Manji refers specifically to al-Andalus, which she describes as "a haven of heterodoxy." It was the time when scholars such as twelfth-century philosopher Ibn Rushd (1126–1198) advocated for the "freedom to reason," and defended women's rights.[12] According to Manji, women, too, were active participants in *ijtihad* and "innovation." One example is the eleventh-century Cordovan poet Wallada bint al-Mustakfi, as Manji explains:

> In the southern Spanish city of Cordoba, for example, a sexually spunky woman named Wallada organized literary salons where people analyzed dreams, poetry, and the Koran. They debated what the Koran proscribed for men and women. But what is a man? And what is a woman? They debated those questions too. The bounty and diversity of Koranic interpretations made this a time in which one could even discuss Islam's implications for hermaphrodites, people born with the genitals of both sexes.[13]

Al-Andalus for Manji is a time when questions about religion and sexuality were not met with death threats and *fatwas*.

In her seminal work *Women and Gender in Islam*, Leila Ahmed also returns to the past as a source of inspiration and feminist hope for Islam. She points to the importance of the feminine in the religious work of thirteenth-century Iberian mystic Ibn 'Arabi (1165–1242). According to Ahmed, Ibn 'Arabi was "probably unique among major Muslim scholars and philosophers in regarding women sympathetically." While she does not attribute his attitude toward women directly to his Andalusi upbringing, Ahmed does not rule it out as a possibility: "The extent to which the different mores of Arab Spain shaped Ibn al-'Arabi's different attitude to women—a question that naturally presents itself at this juncture—has yet to be explored."[14] Yet, if this time period were studied more extensively it might not lead scholars to the answers they are looking for.

Although Mernissi, Manji, and Ahmed have been critical of the patriarchal culture and practices of contemporary Islamic societies, these feminists still hold on to the myth of a Muslim Andalusi society in which women supposedly enjoyed power and sexual emancipation. Such a myth is then strategically used to counter dominant images of present-day subjugation of women under Orthodox Islamic institutions, laws, and practices. Not only does the past offer an alternative to the present, but more importantly, it makes present injustice illegitimate and unnatural, and suggests that a return to an original and authentic Islam embracing of the feminine, even in its theology, would be a return to a more natural state. In this sense, Islamic feminists' return to the past as a source of inspiration and refuge from present society's patriarchal injustices is not different from some Western feminists' own construction of a prehistoric matriarchal paradise lost. [15]

In al-Andalus, Muslim feminists have constructed their own version of a matriarchal prehistory and pre-orthodoxy. In Ibn 'Arabi's interpretation of Islam Ahmed encounters the possibility for a more feminine Allah. In Subh and other empowered women, Mernissi dreams of possibilities denied to women in her own society. In Wallada, Manji reunites with a sexually audacious and defiant Muslim woman at a time when Islamic institutions are suffocating Muslim women's sexuality. But to what extent are these popular assumptions about al-Andalus and Andalusi women true, and to what extent are representations of Andalusi women decontextualized in order to make them fit within an Islamic feminist agenda? Who was this Andalusi woman who continues to fascinate feminists a millennium later?

THE ANDALUSI WOMAN IN CONTEXT: QUEENS, SLAVES, AND THE WOMEN IN BETWEEN

Reading medieval accounts about or in the voice of Andalusi women, it is easy to understand why they have attracted so many scholars. Take for example Subh, the slave of Christian Basque origin, who became one of the most commanding women of her time. Thanks to her proximity to the most powerful men in al-Andalus, Subh came to be influential in Umayyad court politics, first under her husband's reign and then under her son's Hisham II. When al-Hakam II died, leaving his son Hisham II a minor, Subh and her minister (and supposed lover) al-Mansur Ibn Abi 'Amir (b. 938) held political power as Hisham II's regents. It is believed that Subh succeeded in attracting the homosexual caliph by adopting the physical appearance of a *ghulam*, or young man, having a short haircut and wearing pants. Al-Hakam supposedly gave her the masculine name of Ja'far. [16] Mernissi, however, insists that if Subh and other slave women were capable of capturing the caliph's attention in harems full of beautiful women, it was because these women "were particularly well informed about what was going on in the empire, and they were well versed in key areas of knowledge like the history and power of words, being both poets and linguists. Subh was a perfect example of this."[17] Such qualities were especially important for al-Hakam, a caliph known for his patronage of scholarship and learning. Mastery of Arabic language and literature continued to be valuable qualities among the Andalusi aristocracy even after the fall of the Umayyad. Writing in the thirteenth century, the Tunisian Ahmad Ibn Yusuf al-Tifashi (1184–1253) explains in his *Mut'at al-asma' fi 'ilm al-sama'* (Pleasure to the Ears on the Art of Listening [to music]) that slave women educated in Seville and sent to the kings of al-Andalus and the Maghrib were evaluated for their mastery of Arabic, their handwriting, their expertise in playing instruments, and the repertoire of poems and songs they had memorized. These qualities, not just her physical beauty, were what ultimately determined the price of a slave woman.[18] It is therefore important to think about Subh's monetary value as an educated slave when evaluating her degree of emancipation.

Another Andalusi slave who succeeded in attracting a powerful man with her wit and intelligence was I'timad, named al-Rumaykiyya after the man to whom she belonged, Rumayk Ibn Hajjaj. She is famous for her love affair with the poet and king of Seville Abu al-Qasim Muhammad Ibn 'Abbad, known as al-Mu'tamid (1039–1095). It is said that when he was on a promenade by the river with his courtier and advisor Ibn 'Ammar, al-Mu'tamid began reciting a verse and challenged Ibn 'Ammar to complete it. However, before the latter got a chance to comply, I'timad, who was washing clothes on the riverbank, was quick to respond. Thus their love story began. The king of Seville bought her from her owner and the slave became one of the most important women of al-Andalus. During times of prosperity, al-Mu'tamid provided his lover with all the luxury she desired. It is said that when I'timad lamented to the king that she could not see snow from her window, al-Mu'tamid had almond trees planted in the Sierra of Cordoba so that from a distance the falling white blossoms would look like snow. When she expressed her desire to play in the mud barefoot, al-Mu'atmid ordered for the patio to be covered with mud made of musk and sugar so as to fulfill his beloved's wish.[19]

Thanks to their ability to seduce powerful men through both their beauty and intellect, many women in al-Andalus rose from slavery to become powerful queens. In some cases, the daughters of these slaves enjoyed power as part of the aristocratic elite. This was the case of the best known Cordovan woman poet, Wallada Bint al-Mustakfi (d. 1091). Her mother was an Iberian Christian slave and her father, Muhammad III al Mustakfi (r. 1024–1025), was an Umayyad caliph at a time of great political instability. Although relatively little is known about her, she is remembered as a *femme rebelle* thanks primarily to her poems, which are assumed to be autobiographical. She refused to wear the veil, and made a name for herself among the literary and cultural elite of Cordova. It is said that when the supreme judge of Cordova accused her of being a harlot, she responded by embroidering scandalous, defiantly sexual verses on her robe. On the right hand side was written:

> I am, by God, fit for high positions,
> And am going my way, with pride!

While the left side said:

> Forsooth, I allow my lover to touch my cheek,
> And bestow my kiss on him who craves it!

Wallada also used her poems to document both her attachment to and anger toward her lovers, both male and female. In one poem she instructs her lover, presumably the Andalusi poet Ibn Zaydun (1003–1071), as to the time and place of their meeting:

> Be ready to visit me as darkness gathers,
> For I believe that night keeps all secrets best:
> The love I feel for you—did the sun feel it thus—
> It would not shine, moon would not rise, stars would cease travelling!

In another poem, Wallada insults Ibn Zaydun:

> They call you the "Sixer"; and your life will leave you before this
> nickname does:
> Sodomite and buggered you are, adulterer, pimp, cuckold, and
> thief![20]

Upon hearing gossip about his rival Ibn 'Abdus' relationship with Wallada, Ibn Zaydun did not hesitate to respond in his *Diwan* with insults of his own:

> They taunt me that Abu 'Amir frequents her house,
> But the butterfly is attracted to the fire,
> That he has taken my place with the woman I love
> But in this there's no ire
> Appetizing food it was, of which I got the best
> And the rest I left to the mouse.[21]

In the following century, Wallada was remembered with admiration for her dissent from and defiance of the norms of her society. The Andalusi writer Abu al-Hasan Ibn Bassam, who dedicated his book *Kitab al-dakhira fi mahasin ahl al-jazira* (The Treasury of Excellent Qualities of the People of the Peninsula) (1106–1109) to the defense of Andalusi scholars and poets against the assumption that their work was inferior to those in the East,[22] wrote that:

> She was the first of the women of her time. Her free manners and disdain of the veil indicated an ardent nature. This was, however, the best manner to show her remarkable inward qualities, the sweetness of her face and her character. Her house at Cordova was the arena in which poets and prose writers were vying with each other. The literary

men were attracted toward the light of this brilliant new moon, as if it were a lighthouse in a dark night. The greatest poets and prose writers were anxious to obtain the sweetness of her intimacy, which it was not difficult to attain.[23]

The fascinating life of Wallada, as it has been constructed in the poems attributed to her as well as in the writing of her contemporaries and later Andalusi and Maghribi chroniclers, has made her one of the most recognizable Andalusi figures in the Muslim world today. In a beautiful neighborhood of Casablanca, Morocco, a high school is named after her, Lycée Ouallada, which was, until recently, a girls-only institution. Wallada has continued to be celebrated as the symbol of Muslim women's emancipation even beyond the western Mediterranean. One of the earliest Saudi poetic plays was *The Passion of Wallada* by Husain 'Abdallah Siraj, about the life and loves of the Cordovan princess.[24]

The stories of these women go against how one imagines the place of women in medieval Muslim society. However, it is also important to remember that Wallada was an exception in al-Andalus: there are few stories of women like her. In addition to her wealth, what allowed Wallada to become what she is celebrated for, namely a daring Muslim woman, sexually aggressive and defiant of conventions, is also the absence of a strong male figure whose *'ird*, or honor, was going to be tainted by her promiscuity. She was not married and her father was too consumed with political turmoil to care about his daughter's comportment. Similarly, the power and "freedom" that Subh and I'timad supposedly enjoyed was the result of their status as slaves, and as such, these women's sexual promiscuity did not represent a danger to a male relative. This explains why most love stories and sexual anecdotes in medieval Arabo-Muslim literature involve slave women. A "free" Muslim woman's chastity is important to establishing a man's honor. Declaring love for a free woman could be lethal. Confessing publicly one's love for a slave woman, on the other hand, does not have the same implications since she is a man's property, and as such, he has the right to enjoy her without endangering another man's honor. As Manuela Marín explains, "Young and childless slave girls were the privileged object of love expression in Andalusi literature, and they are, too, the only women whose feelings are openly recorded. Men who would never dream of declaring their love for the female members of a peer's family could show publicly their attachment to their slaves, who, for their part, developed occasionally strong ties of affection with their masters."[25] Knowing her relationships (or lack thereof) with men and keeping the historical context in mind, it may be more fitting to view Wallada as an exception rather than the norm.

One should be careful, however, not to fetishize or exaggerate the slave woman's supposed emancipation. It is important to keep in mind the violence that brought women such as Subh, I'timad, and even Wallada's mother into the palaces of powerful and wealthy men. There were different ways through which a slave entered the court. Many slaves were acquired as booty in war. Others were purchased; the price varied depending on many factors including their knowledge and education. As mentioned earlier, the thirteenth-century scholar al-Tifashi wrote about the reality of trade in educated slaves in al-Andalus and North Africa. While aristocratic men and even women have praised their young, beautiful slaves for their intellect and singing ability, and while scholars today such as Mernissi have celebrated and idealized love between caliphs and their slaves, it is important to remember what Michelle Hamilton has termed "the ugly reality of the Andalusi sex trade."[26] The education of slaves was a lucrative business for the seller, providing a luxurious product for the pleasure of wealthy buyers. Once in the house of their master, these women had to compete for his attention. Becoming the favorite and giving birth to a son could open the door to power and financial security, as it did for Subh and I'timad. Because there was so much to gain, women went to extremes to secure proximity to the Caliph. In one instance, a slave paid the Caliph's wife to allow her to have sex with her husband.[27] In another instance, the competition among women for the Caliph's attention led to violence, even murder.[28] Securing a position close to the Caliph did not guarantee a slave woman's safety. They were always at the risk of punishment and physical violence at the hand of their masters.[29] One is left wondering if, in circumstances in which women are entirely at the mercy of men, one can refer to love? Does it even make sense to speak of love between a *jariya* and her Caliph?

In addition to their status as free or slaves, another factor to take into consideration when discussing Andalusi women is socio-economic class. So far, the discussion has centered on women from the elite, as is the case in most studies about Andalusi women. As Marín has pointed out, Andalusi texts on which today's scholars rely to construct al-Andalus and its women do not tell a complete story since they usually reflect the views and cater to the desires of a privileged urban masculine elite.[30] The majority of women in al-Andalus, as in the rest of the medieval Muslim world, were not part of that class. Most slaves in al-Andalus, as Carlos Alberto Montaner has pointed out, were used for domestic service. Even those whose beauty and intellect assured them entry into a powerful man's harem, ended up, when they aged, in service as, for example, nannies to the harem's younger children. Furthermore, Montaner counters the celebratory discourse of slave women in the Muslim world by pointing to the abuse and violence to which they were routinely subjected: "Though the Koran forbade mistreating and assaulting captives, there were frequent flagellations, mutilations (usually of nose and ears), and fatal incidents of dragging prisoners tethered to horses."[31] Though education and intelligence were valued in these women, there is still reason to be skeptical when speaking of the supposed liberation of slaves.

Andalusi women included not merely aristocrats or slaves but also active participants in nearly every aspect of society. Although their economic contributions did not equal those of men, especially considering the restrictions imposed on them in public spaces, women still participated in many professions. As Ibn Hazm tells us, Andalusi women were doctors, teachers, hairdressers, hired mourners, matchmakers, thieves, seamstresses, and weavers.[32] Some succeeded in the publishing industry, mainly as copyists.[33] Muslim women could also be criminals, from thieves to apostates, as in the case of Flora. Born to a Muslim man and a Christian woman, Flora was secretly raised Christian by her mother after her father's death. Eventually, Flora declared her Christianity publicly, for which she was arrested and decapitated on November 24, 851.[34]

These other Andalusi women, to whom history has dedicated few if any pages at all, thus find themselves doubly silenced. Today, they are silenced in feminist scholarship, their lives and experiences glamorized in order to cater to the fantasies of their inventors. In the past, they were silenced by the pre-modern scholars who were interested only in elite women, women who were actively engaged in the pleasuring of men, physically or intellectually. One exception, however, is the exalted twelfth-century Cordovan philosopher Ibn Rushd (1126–1198), known in the West as Averroes. In his writing, Ibn Rushd lamented the situation of women in his society:

> The competence of women is unknown, however, in these cities since they are only taken (in them) for procreation and hence are placed at the service of their husbands and confined to procreation, upbringing, and suckling. This nullifies their [other] activities. Since women in these cities are not prepared with respect to any of the human virtues, they frequently resemble plants in these cities. Their being a burden upon the men (in these cities) is one of the causes of the poverty of these cities. This is because they are to be found there in double the number of men, while not understanding through [their] upbringing any of the necessary actions except for the few actions—like the art of spinning and weaving—that they undertake mostly at a time when they have need of them to make up for their lack of spending (power).[35]

The fact that the prominent Islamic jurist Ibn Rushd denounces the limits imposed on women in spite of his deep knowledge of religion, law, and philosophy may seem revolutionary. In fact, Moroccan scholar Hasna Lebbady describes him as a "feminist *avant la lettre*."[36] She compares his writings to those of eighteenth-century British feminist writer Mary Wollstonecraft (1759–1797), who expressed concerns about women like Ibn Rushd's, except that, in the words of Lebbady, he did so "some six hundred years" earlier. Similarly, Manji celebrates Ibn Rushd as the philosopher who "championed the [. . .] freedom to reason" and who dared "to differ with the theocrats."[37] However, it is important to point that Ibn

Rushd was more of an exception in the mostly conservative Iberia. In fact, he was exiled and his books were burned.

Reading Andalusi women in context exposes the limits of their supposed emancipation. Andalusi women were a heterogeneous group, and while women such as Wallada ought to be included in the telling of a more complete history of the experience of Muslim women in medieval Iberia, it is erroneous to use her to "represent" the Andalusi woman. Despite her audacious writings and a school for girls that bears her name, history does not record a direct influence by Wallada over the women of her time. Her work did not resonate within a community of freely creative women and men because such a community did not exist. It is undeniable that there were Andalusi women who were powerful, rich, independent, and sexually promiscuous. Nevertheless, the reality is that the majority of women in al-Andalus, as in the rest of the medieval world, lived under a patriarchal hegemony and endured its inherent injustice. These are the women who expose the limits of the myth of al-Andalus.

THE ANDALUSI MAN IN CONTEXT: WAR, SEX, AND QUEER ANXIETIES

Like Andalusi women, Muslim Andalusi men are a heterogeneous group made up of aristocrats, slaves, and all those in between. Like Andalusi women, all of them were affected by military conflict. In an attempt to present al-Andalus as a paradise of *convivencia*, it is sometimes forgotten that it was also the scene of constant military conflict. These wars had an impact on all aspects of Andalusi life, including literary production and, in particular, the ways in which men portrayed women. One of these, which has fascinated academics and non-academics alike, is the proliferation of writing about sex in the medieval Muslim world, and in al-Andalus and North Africa in particular. Take for example the following *kharja* in which the feminine poetic voice explicitly refers to her preferred sexual position:

> I won't make love to you
> except with one condition:
> that you lift my ankle-bracelets
> to my earrings![38]

The fact that such words are uttered in a feminine voice can be perhaps shocking to a reader accustomed to today's dominant images of passive Muslim women peeking from behind a burqa. However, it is important to remember that while composed in the voice of a woman, most of these and other erotic poems are written by men for a predominantly male audience.[39] The men of this audience did not necessarily have easy access to women because of the segregation of women from men; thus, one can easily think of such poems as fulfilling a pornographic function.[40] At the same time since men were frequently absent, primarily at war or jihad, these poems also expose men's profound anxiety about women's sexual agency.

Jihad, or lawful military warfare against infidels and apostates, was understood in the Middle Ages as the duty of all able-bodied (physically and mentally) Muslims as clearly stated in the Qur'an, the *hadith*, and scholarly commentaries. Jihad earns one religious prestige and the promise of reward in the afterlife.[41] In patriarchal Arab-Muslim society, jihad came to be a way through which men reaffirmed their masculinity and virility. In the Sura of al-Tawba (Repentance), those who chose to stay behind (*yatakhallafun*) instead of following Muhammad to war are looked down upon (9:120), as were those who asked to stay behind (9:49). In al-Nisa' (Women) it is made clear that there is a hierarchy among believers. In contrast to the effeminate *qawa'id*, literally the sitting ones, or those who remain at home without a valid excuse, are the superior and masculine *mujahidun* (warriors of jihad) who sacrifice their comfort, wealth, and lives for the sake of Allah (4:95).[42] Jihad is, essentially, an idealized version of masculine bravery and honor, a vision that does not necessarily include women.

Knowing these connotations of jihad, one is left wondering if the fact that these *mujahidun* had to leave for war provoked masculine anxieties over abandoning women without a masculine authority figure to guard them and prevent their *nushuz* or rebellion. Fears about what women did in their absence was a constant source of preoccupation for Muslim men in general, and theologians in particular.[43] In fact, one of the early justifications for polygamy was to see it as a remedy to the shortage of men due to war. According to this argument, polygamy allowed women to enter into marriage in order to gain relative economic stability but also to prevent the *fitna* (chaos) that would ensue if women's sexuality were unrestrained. Moreover, the Qur'an provides advice to men on how to deal with women whose *nushuz* could be a threat.[44] Muslim Andalusi jurists and theologians expressed their fear of women's behavior in the absence of a male authority, both in public and private. For example, in his *hisba* manual Ibn 'Abdun (d.1134) insists on the need to separate women from men.[45] In his famous *Tawq al-hamama* (*The Ring of the Dove*) the legal scholar and theologian Ibn Hazm (d.1064), who lived in a period of great political turbulence, documents the behavior of women he himself voyeuristically observed while living in his father's harem until the age of fourteen. He writes: "I forget nothing of what I have seen them do. This all springs from a profound jealousy innate in me, and a deep suspicion of women's ways." Ibn Hazm insists that because of their feeble intellect, if not controlled and occupied, women turn to sex: "they [women] have nothing else to fill their minds, except a loving union and what brings it about, flirting and how it is done, intimacy and the various ways of achieving it. This is their sole occupation, and they were created for nothing else."[46]

The jealousy that pushed Ibn Hazm to document women's transgressions is repeatedly evoked in the Andalusi *kharja* in the voices of women who fear their male lovers' violence:

> My man is violently jealous; he hurts me.
> If I go out, he will harm me—
> I can't make a move or he threatens me.
> Mamma, tell me what to do![47]

While this *kharja* expresses the feminine voice's fright at the idea of transgressing, other poems cater to a masculine voyeuristic desire to witness what women do in the absence of men, recurring to entertaining sexual humor so as to feed and justify patriarchal distrust of women. In a twelfth-century *kharja*, the feminine poetic voice calls on her lover in the absence of her husband:

> My little lover, be resolute.
> Rise and attack me.
> Kiss my mouth,
> come and embrace my breast
> and raise my anklets up to my earrings.
> My husband is busy.[48]

In another *kharja*, the feminine poetic voice offers herself sexually to a returning soldier:

> Seducer! Shameless seducer!
> O, come back here again—
> and rest with me, take your ease,
> after your hard soldiering.[49]

While in yet another *kharja* a woman takes advantage of her husband's injury to sneak in a lover:

> my beloved, my beloved, come in to me
> when my husband lies wounded.[50]

It is not possible to establish with certainty the cause of absence of men in specific *kharjas*, though it is likely that the injury to which the poetic voice refers is one endured in a military conflict. It is a fact that wars against both Muslim and Christian opponents forced men of different socio-economic classes to be away from their homes, and in the case of the wealthy, their harems. War, however, was not the only reason why men were absent from their homes for a period of time. Thanks to al-Andalus' vibrant economy, it was also common for Andalusi merchants to conduct long-distance trade that took them away from their homes for weeks, even months.[51] Nevertheless, regardless of the specific reason, it appears that such absences, along with distrust of women, triggered male anxiety that influenced the way Andalusi men represented women.

One key example of such anxiety is the thirteenth-century Andalusi tale, *Hadith Bayad wa Riyad*. Cynthia Robinson has suggested that because of its depiction of "frivolous" themes, it is possible that the text was "anti-, or extra-Almohad." The tale, in her view, could have been produced in one of the courts of the Almohads' opponents, following the Almohads' loss of power, particularly after the battle of Las Navas de Tolosa (1212).[52] Robinson's hypothesis is further confirmed by the text's depiction of women who have deviated from their "natural" roles and the impotent men who fail to control them.[53] At first glance, and particularly given the title by which the text came to be known, *Hadith Bayad wa Riyad* appears to be just another love story, in this case between Bayad, the son of a Damascene merchant, and Riyad, the favorite slave girl of a wealthy and powerful *hajib* (high ranking government official). The story is narrated by the *'ajuz* (old woman) who is also the lovers' go-between. Bayad falls in love with Riyad while on a promenade by the *hajib*'s home. Taking advantage of the *hajib*'s absence, his daugher, the *Sayyida* (Lady), the *'ajuz*, Bayad, Riyad, and several other women meet in the palace's garden. After much drinking and singing, Riyad openly admits her love for Bayad. At such a confession, the *Sayyida* violently puts an end to the party, ripping her own dress and accusing Riyad of being ungrateful. The *'ajuz* and Bayad exit the palace, the latter covered by a veil to pass for a woman. A period of separation between the two lovers follows, during which the *Sayyida* imprisons Riyad to punish her, but eventually forgives her. In the meantime, Bayad and Riyad continue to communicate through letters. The text concludes with the promise of another reunion in the *Sayyida*'s garden to which the *'ajuz* and Bayad are invited. The reader, however, cannot know what happens next, since the first and last folios are damaged.

Except for the opening scene in which the reader finds the *hajib* in the company of the *'ajuz* and his girl slaves, the regulating influence of the *hajib* remains absent for the remainder of the text. As a government official during a period of war among Muslims (the Almohad and others) and between Muslims and Christians, it is likely that the *hajib* is away at war.[54] There is no doubt in the text as to the power that he should have over the women. For example, fearing her father's punishment, the *Sayyida* asks Bayad not to reveal anything about what he witnesses during the gathering.[55] Yet such fear does not seem to deter or even curtail the women's transgressions. The ease with which women "smuggle" Bayad into the palace indicates that it is not the first time a man has entered the *hajib*'s home in the latter's absence. Medieval readers would have been amused by the *hajib*'s habitual failures to control his daughter and slaves. The role the *hajib* plays in the text, or rather, the role he fails to play, contradicts the literal meaning of the term *hajib*, which shares the same root as *hijab,* or veil, literally meaning the veiler or concealer. According to Mernissi, the verse of the *hijab* in the Qur'an resulted from a concern with tact: "He [Allah] wanted to intimate to the Companions [of the prophet Mohammed] certain niceties that they seemed to lack, like not entering a dwelling without asking permission."[56] In other words, and as Mernissi proposes, the *hijab's* function is to delimit one's private space in order to effect a separation between two men, which makes Bayad's recurrent entries into the garden particularly ironic.

Similarly, the other main male character, Bayad, appears to be unimportant since the main events of the story, including its crisis and resolution, revolve around two women: the *Sayyida* and Riyad. Even though the *Sayyida* feels torn between fear of her father and love for Riyad, in the end she succumbs to Riyad's desire. The reconciliation scene is represented in both the narrative and the illustration. The illustration depicts the *Sayyida* sitting as usual on her throne with Riyad prostrating herself in front of her, the rest of the women standing behind the throne. In the narrative, however, the hierarchy is not quite clear. The *Sayyida* repeats once again that if she grants Riyad's desire it is not because she wishes to unite her with her lover but rather because she fears losing her. As Riyad falls asleep drunk in the *Sayyida's* lap, the latter "brushed her hair from her cheeks and kissed her between the eyes, over her heart, and on her cheeks."[57] Bayad is only reintroduced back into the palace after order has been reestablished. In this sense, the uniform title given to the text, *Hadith Bayad wa Riyad* is misleading, for it situates the Andalusi tale within the Arabic literary tradition of reciprocated love between a man and a woman, similar to the canonic pair Qays and Layla. In the Andalusi tale however, women take over the stage, even when it comes to love, while men are marginalized and ridiculed. Thus in spite of its light love poems and colorful images, *Hadith Bayad wa Riyad* reveals the author's mistrust of women and his anxiety that in the absence of men, women are sexually promiscuous and even capable of subverting heterosexual norms.

This contextualized reading of a depiction of same-sex desire goes against recent celebratory trends in scholarship about medieval Islamic portrayals of homosexuality. The leading scholar of female homosexuality in the literature of the Muslim world is Samar Habib, whose work has sought to demonstrate that homosexual relationships between Arab women have existed and have been documented from at least as early as the 9th century. Habib refers to texts such as *Rushd al-labib ila mu'asharat al-habib* (An Intelligent Man's Guide to the Art of Coition) by al-Yemeni (d. 850) in which the author includes a love story between two women, Hind and her lover, known as the daughter of Hassan. Al-Yemeni describes how Hind, who was "the best of the folks of her time, she was completely without excesses," falls prey to manipulation by Hassan's daughter: "The daughter of Hassan did not cease to deceive her [Hind] and to decorate grinding for her and to say: In the union of two women

there is a pleasure that cannot be between the woman and the man."
Hind is sold when she has sex with the daughter of Hassan: "Hind found
a pleasure that was even greater than the other had described and their
amorous desire for each other increased—and it had never been so between women before this." When the daughter of Hassan dies, Hind is so
devastated that she "sat at her grave all the time until people began to use
her case for their sayings. Al-Farzdak said: 'I was devoted to you in a
time that you bestowed kindly/Like Hind was devoted to Hassan Yama-
ni's daughter.'"[58]

Habib employs this and other anecdotes about lesbians in medieval
Islamic texts, particularly al-Tifashi's thirteenth-century treatise *Nuzhat
al-albab fima la yujadu fi kitab* (The Delight of Hearts, or What You Will Not
Find in Any Book), as examples of Muslim scholars' positive depiction of
same-sex love. Habib's agenda is to counter today's homophobia in the
Muslim world by inviting Muslims to re-examine their own Islamic heritage, reassuring them that lesbians are not a Western invention and that
in fact, not only are they part of Islamic history, they are even embraced
by Islam's most prominent theologians and jurists. Habib is not alone in
her quest to educate Muslims about their sexual past. Algerian-French
intellectual Malek Chebel repeats incessantly that Islam does not condemn women's sexuality in all its forms. As he explained in a recent
interview about Islam and sexuality, "Dans les premiers temps, la sexual-
ité, la passion amoureuse et le plaisir n'étaient pas des thèmes tabous et
on en débattait librement, y compris dans les sphères religieuses." ("In
the early days, sexuality, passion, love and pleasure were not taboo top-
ics and were freely debated, even within religious spheres.") He refers to
Islam's "temps des Lumières," or enlightenment, when women's and
men's sexuality was not taboo and when poets and scholars such as Abu
Nuwas, al-Mas'udi, and al-Jahiz wrote about sex without censure.[59]
Along the same lines, Tunisian intellectual Abdelwahab Bouhdiba la-
ments today's "misogynistic" Muslim societies that have deviated from
Islam's original message: "How far we are from the feminism of the
Quran!"[60] Bouhdiba, too, celebrates premodern sexual treatises such as
Sheikh al-Nafzawi's *Al-Rawd al-'atir fi nuzhat al-khatir* (The Perfumed Garden) which, he insists, "belongs to authentic Islamic tradition."[61] Furthermore, every couple of years, the liberal French-language Moroccan magazine *TelQuel: Le Maroc tel qu'il est* publishes an article on sex in Islam's
golden past. In "Erotisme: Quand les musulmans osaient," the Moroccan
journalist Driss Ksikes gives an overview of medieval sexual treatises in
which scholars such as al-Tifashi and al-Nafzawi "dared" to celebrate
women and their sexuality.[62] More recently, another article appeared,
"Saphisme, homosexualité, plaisirs défendus: L'histoire insoupçonnée de
l'érotisme en terre d'Islam," in which once again, the stories of lesbians,
homosexual men, and other lovers are told to support the idea that in the

past, sex in all its forms was viewed as a positive and integral part of Muslim women and men's experiences.[63]

Such conclusions, however, are based on a partial or selective reading of these medieval texts. While certain passages may appear to be favorable to women, the primary thrust of these treatises remains a fundamental concern with men's well-being and their distrust of women. Sheikh al-Nafzawi, who is celebrated by Bouhdiba as the author of an authentically Islamic treatise, and whose work Tariq Ali salutes as a "biting critique of religious hypocrisy,"[64] discusses at length women's constant longing and obsession with sex. He has a chapter "On the Deceits and Treacheries of Women," in which he insists that women, like Satan, are not to be trusted. He provides numerous examples of how they are constantly employing ruses to take advantage of unsuspecting men. Moreover, women in al-Nafzawi's narrative will do anything for pleasure, including having sex with animals.[65]

Such statements should not come as a surprise. It bears repeating that these works are by male authors writing primarily for a male audience. They have two priorities: to entertain men and to educate them through both negative and positive examples. Far from challenging the Islamic patriarchal order, theologians and jurists seek to reinforce it. For this reason these authors never shy away from misogynistic remarks. Furthermore, although these authors wrote in such an explicit manner about sexuality, it does not automatically follow that they were any less orthodox or misogynistic. The large majority of these theologians and jurists went to great lengths to justify their endeavors and convince their readers of the legitimacy of their sexual writings. Ibn Hazm, for example, insists that "Many rightly-guided caliphs and orthodox imams have been lovers."[66] "But to admire beauty, and to be mastered by love," he explains, is "a natural thing." The Muslim man's duty, however, is "to abstain from those things which Allah has forbidden," or else his actions will be "charged to his account on the day of Resurrection." [67] These sorts of contradictions are precisely what make the history of al-Andalus less a "Golden Age" of *convivencia*, and more likely a complicated era in need of serious academic attention.

AL-ANDALUS: AN "ENNOBLING LIE"

What is wrong with myth? What is the harm in inventing al-Andalus and the medieval past in general as a time and place in which women were powerful and sex was positive? Why not use the past to educate and even inspire Muslims to create a tolerant and just society respectful of women's rights? The problem with the Andalusi myth is not simply its falsehood, but the implications of such falsehood for a feminist agenda. Like other feel-good myths, it functions as what Kwame Anthony Appiah has termed an "ennobling lie"; it satisfies a yearning for a time *before* "blank," whatever that "blank" may be, but as a lie it can have dangerous consequences.[68] In *The Myth of Matriarchal Prehistory: Why an Invented Past Won't Give Women a Future*, historian of religion Cynthia Eller casts doubt on the historical veracity and "feminist utility" of the myth of matriarchy, mentioned earlier in this chapter, which feminists including Gloria Steinem have used very much as Islamic feminists use the myth of al-Andalus, to suggest that there was a time *before* sexism and patriarchy. While wishful and comforting, this understanding of history is ultimately unproductive. As Eller puts it, "If we are certain that we want to get rid of sexism, we do not need a mythical time of women's past greatness to get on with the effort toward ending it." Eller concludes her book by stating that:

> Feminist matriarchal myth does not actually recount the history of sexism, as it purports to do. It may provide us with a vision of what it considers to be socially desirable and the hope that it can be attained. But we do not need matriarchal myth to tell us that sexism is bad or that change is possible. With the help of all feminists, matriarchalist and otherwise, we need to decide what we want and set about getting it. Next to this, the "knowledge" that we once had it will pale into insignificance.[69]

In the same way that Eller questions the feminist utility of the Western feminist matriarchy myth, one ought to challenge the feminist utility of Islamic feminists' use of the Andalusi myth. Beyond the propagation of historical falsehoods, the Andalusi myth is unproductive and even dangerous for five reasons:

(1) The myth of al-Andalus is a distraction. Most educated young women growing up in a country such as Morocco for example have heard about Andalusi woman poet Umayyad Wallada; some of them even have studied in one of the many schools named after famous women from the past.[70] It is ironic that while in the West scholars often complain about the fact that women's achievements have been left out of history, in the Muslim world, including in countries as conservative as Saudi Arabia, women from the past are still celebrated today. Such recognition of medieval women, however, does not spring out of a feminist consciousness. If anything, the past is usually used to silence women in the present. In response to feminist demands in Muslim countries, the usual answer is that Islam already granted women all their rights at a time when women in the West had none. Wallada, Subh, I'timad, and others are given as confirmation of "authentic" Islam's ability to empower women. Hence rather than engage in the kind of daring and unapologetic questioning whose purpose is to secure women's rights and achieve equality, intellectual energy is directed, rather, toward the celebration of an invented past, a celebration that, at best, produces a feel-good benefit.

(2) The myth of al-Andalus exposes the limits of Islamic feminism, a point that is further elaborated in chapters 3 and 4 to come. The myth of al-Andalus reinforces the belief that there is an "authentic" message from which Muslims have deviated and to which they ought to return. This is summarized in the often repeated claim that the "problem" is not Islam but rather Muslims themselves. Such a statement puts religion above blame, making injustices that Muslim women endure in the name of Islam the result of human misunderstanding of the true doctrine. Any reform achieved in this sense would only target the surface since the textual core is always put above blame or critique. Ironically, the need for a "return" to authenticity is precisely what people such as Osama Bin Laden have called for. Bin Laden even named al-Andalus in his speeches, lamenting its loss and calling for jihad in order to restore legitimately Muslim territories "from Palestine to al-Andalus and other Islamic lands that were lost because of the betrayals of rulers and the feebleness of Muslims."[71] In this sense, even though *The New York Times* has called Irshad Manji "Osama Bin Laden's worst nightmare," her call for a return to an authentic uncorrupted source is neither new nor revolutionary.[72]

(3) To aviod interrogating the Self, blame is directed at the West. Once it has been established that tolerant and just societies such as al-Andalus did in fact exist, critique is turned to "foreign" influence that corrupted Muslims and caused them to deviate from their origin. Both injustice toward women and Islamic fundamentalism are blamed on Western colonialism and imperialism. It has even been argued that Muslim men were supposedly forced into hiding Muslim women because of the Western man's voyeuristic gaze.[73] While it is undeniable that colonialism had, and to a certain extent continues to have, a devastating impact in various parts of the world, it does not hold sole culpability for women's secondary status in Muslim societies. Moreover, if, rather than engage in self-criticism, Muslims always blame the West for problems related to women in Muslim societies, how can there be reform?

(4) Another danger of the myth of al-Andalus is that it produces a narcissistic understanding of history that does not benefit women. While the West is still struggling to recognize its medieval Islamic heritage, in the Muslim world Islam's contribution to the emergence of the West is exaggerated to the point of being counterproductive. The West is imagined as originally inferior and eternally indebted to the Muslim world, thus reinforcing the gap between Muslims and the West. Muslims are not solely responsible for such discourse. Oblivious to the nuances, some scholars, overtaken by nostalgia, recount tales of Islam's superiority to the Christian West, as we hear in David William Foster's declaration: "The Arabic civilization of al-Andalus was a pleasure-loving and tolerant culture, destroyed by the conquering Christian civilization of the North."[74] While this kind of discourse caters to the patriarchal ego, Muslim women do not benefit from such supposed superiority to the West.

Wallada, though impressive for her time, is not an appropriate model for Muslim women living in the twenty-first century. Women in the Muslim world and women in the West share, to a certain extent, similar struggles and oppression, which they have endured in the name of religion, honor, and other social constructs. The West, however, has a longer feminist tradition; thus, rather than claim superiority behind veils of insecurities, Muslim women can benefit from the feminist struggles, strategies, and successes of Western feminists.

(5) One of the most dangerous consequences of the myth of al-Andalus is its ethical implications. How can academics make a case for an Andalusi "Golden Age" for women knowing the reality of women today in the Muslim world? While an Andalusi myth is being celebrated, women and sexual minorities are enduring the wrath of modern Islamic orthodoxy. Honor killings and various forms of injustice are still committed, in front of witnesses, in many parts of the Muslim world; they are used to punish a woman who endangers a man's *'ird*, or honor. Today throughout the Muslim world women are being castigated for engaging in sexual acts considered illicit, and even for speaking or writing about sexuality.[75] Similarly, when it comes to the question of homosexuality and Islam, one ought to question the ethical implications of suggesting that women's homosexuality and homosexuality in general was accepted, even celebrated, in the Andalusi "Golden Age", when in fact the laws that condemn homosexuality today in the Muslim world, which is punishable in some instances by death, are inspired by the same religious texts that shaped the views of Andalusi jurists such as Ibn Hazm. [76] The Andalusi myth is holding back Muslim women as well as other sexual minorities in the Muslim world, and rather than celebrate the falsehood that is the "Golden Age" it is time for academics to move beyond myths and invest their energy in more useful endeavors.

For centuries, al-Andalus has been celebrated as the time and place in which theology, sexuality, and women's emancipation were not mutually exclusive. The rhetoric of the Andalusi woman's emancipation appeals to Western scholars and reform-minded Islamic feminists, who celebrate Andalusi women's sexual agency as a time before corruption by Islamic fundamentalists and the West. Nevertheless, as this chapter demonstrates, not only does the myth of al-Andalus promote falsehood about the place of women in medieval Andalusi society and in Andalusi men's imagination, it is also a myth that has dangerous implications for Muslim women today as it stands between them and the possibility of a meaningful reform.

The following chapter addresses falsehoods about the place of Muslim women in Western representations. While women's agency is exaggerated in representations by Muslim writers and artists, Western representations, on the other hand, are seen as constructing an image of a passive Muslim woman at the mercy of an oppressive Muslim man. This chapter will introduce a large corpus of premodern Western literature from different geographic areas and various periods that suggest more nuance in the Western understandings of Islam and Muslim women.

NOTES

1. Victor Hernández Cruz, *In the Shadow of al-Andalus: Poems* (Minneapolis: Coffee House Press, 2011), xi.

2. María Rosa Menocal, *The Ornament of the World: How Muslims, Jews, and Christians Created a Culture of Tolerance in Medieval Spain* (New York: Little Brown, 2002), 283.

3. For a discussion of how Juan Goytisolo has been influenced by the theories of Américo Castro see Michael Ugarte, "Juan Goytisolo: Unruly Disciple of Américo Castro," *Journal of Spanish Studies: Twentieth Century* 7 (1979): 353–64. On Goytisolo's construction and adaptation of al-Andalus in his work, see Claudia Schaefer-Rodríguez, *Juan Goytisolo: del 'realismo crítico' a la utopía* (Madrid: Porrúa Turranzas, 1984).

4. A copy of the speech can be accessed at http://www.msnbc.msn.com/id/31098535/ns/politics-white_house/t/obama-seeks-new-beginning-muslim-world/#. TuQf0nNW6xE (4 June 2012).

5. Scholars such as Bat Ye'or have questioned the myth of a peaceful *convivencia*; see for example Bat Ye'or, *The Dhimmi: Jews and Christians under Islam*, trans. David Maisel, Paul Fenton, and David Littman (Rutherford: Fairleigh Dickinson University Press, 1985). However, the myth continues to be popular. Menocal's bestselling *Ornament of the World* is a case in point. It is even included in the "Islam Reference List" of books on the website of the Philadelphia chapter of the conservative Council on American-Islamic Relations (CAIR) http://pa.cair.com/education/islam-reference-list/. In fiction and, as Daniela Flesler has pointed out, historical writing centering on the theme of Andalusi *convivencia* has become a genre. For example, the prolific novelist Magdalena Lasala has made a career out of telling idealized narratives of famous Andalusi figures such as Wallada. For more on Lasala's historical novels, see Flesler, *The Return of the Moor: Spanish Responses to Contemporary Moroccan Immigration* (West Lafayette: Purdue University Press, 2008), 115–20. Moreover, it is not coincidental that one of the recent costly additions to Metropolitan Museum of Art in New York City was an Andalusi-Maghribi courtyard built by Moroccan artisans.

6. As David Ringrose has pointed out, the myth of *convivencia* has been revived in Spanish political rhetoric as "a medieval tradition of pluralism which supposedly survived in spite of foreign absolutism and Inquisition." Ringrose, *Spain, Europe, and the "Spanish miracle", 1700–1900* (Cambridge: Cambridge University Press, 1996), 5.

7. Thomas Friedman, for example, is not convinced by the division between Islam and Muslims: "but you keep telling us what Islam isn't. You need to tell us what it is and show us how its positive interpretations are being promoted in your schools and mosques. If this is not Islam, then why is it that a million Muslims will pour into the streets to protest Danish cartoons of the Prophet Muhammad, but not one will take to the streets to protest Muslim suicide bombers who blow other Muslims, real people, created in the image of God?" "America vs. The Narrative." *New York Times* 28 Nov. 2009: Op-ed page. *New York Times*, available at http://www.nytimes.com/2009/11/29/opinion/29friedman.html (4 June 2012).

8. Menocal, *Ornament of the World*, xv.

9. "L'Andalousie" is a motif in the writings of Ben Jelloun and Djebar, idealized as a space to which these postcolonial writers escape from the orthodoxies of Islam and Western colonialism. This is particularly evident in Djebar's *Vast est la prison* (Paris: Albin Michel, 1995) and Ben Jelloun's *L'enfant de sable* (Paris: Editions du Seuil, 1985). For a discussion of the place of al-Andalus in contemporary Arabic literature, see

Pedro Martínez Montávez, *Al-Andalus, España, en la literature árabe contemporánea: La casa del pasado* (Madrid: MAPERE, 1992).

10. On the increase of anti-semitism in Muslim countries, see Robert S. Wistrich, *Muslim Anti-Semitism: A Clear and Present Danger* (New York: American Jewish Committee, 2002).

11. Fatima Mernissi, *The Forgotten Queens of Islam*, trans. Mary Jo Lakeland (Minneapolis: University of Minnesota Press, 1993). The original French version was published in 1990 under the title: *Sultanes oubliées: femmes chefs d'état en Islam (Forgotten Sultans: Women Heads of State in Islam.)*

12. Manji, *The Trouble with Islam: A Muslim's Call for Reform in Her Faith* (New York: St. Martin's Press, 2003), 55–56.

13. Ibid., 51–52.

14. Ahmed, *Women and Gender in Islam*, 99–100.

15. For example, see Elizabeth Gould Davis, *The First Sex* (New York: Putman, 1971) and Gloria Steinem, *Wonder Woman* (New York: Holt, Rinehart and Winston, 1972).

16. It is also possible that Subh dressed like a man because it gave her better access to men's world. Mernissi tells the story of another woman, Radiyya, the daughter of Sultan Iltutmish, king of Delhi. According to premodern Arab sources, after the death of her father, Radiyya cut her hair and wore men's clothing, which allowed her to engage in activities such as leading military campaigns, and facilitated communication with her male subjects. *Forgotten Queens of Islam*, 96.

17. Ibid., 46–47.

18. For an English translation of the passage addressing slave women's education, see Benjamin Liu and James Monroe, *Ten Hispano-Arabic Strophic Songs in the Modern Oral Tradition: Music and Texts*, University of California Publications in Modern Philology, 125 (Berkeley: University of California Press, 1989), 37–38.

19. Anwar Chejne, *Muslim Spain: Its History and Culture* (St. Paul: University of Minnesota Press, 1974), 249–50.

20. Translated in Devin Stewart, "Ibn Zaydun," in *The Cambridge History of Arabic Literature: The Literature of al-Andalus*, ed. Maria Rosa Menocal and Michael Sells (Cambridge: Cambridge University Press, 2000), 309.

21. Translated in Salma Khadra Jayyusi, "Andalusi Poetry: The Golden Period," in *The Legacy of Muslim Spain*, ed. Jayyusi (Leiden: E. J. Brill, 1992), 349.

22. See Otto Zwartjes, *Love songs from al-Andalus: History, Structure, and Meaning of the Kharja* (Leiden: E. J. Brill, 1997), 42–45.

23. Excerpt from Ibn Bassam translated in Alois Nykl, *Hispano-Arabic Poetry and its Relations With Old Provençal Troubadours* (Baltimore: J. H. Furst, 1946), 107.

24. Very little has been written about this Saudi play. See Al-Hazimi, Mansour, Ezzat Khattab, and Salma Khadra Jayyusi, ed., *Beyond the Dunes: An Anthology of Modern Saudi Literature* (New York: I. B. Tauris, 2006), 37.

25. See Manuela Marín, "Marriage and Sexuality in al-Andalus," in *Marriage and Sexuality in Medieval and Early Modern Iberia*, ed. Eukene Lacarra Lanz (New York: Routledge, 2002), 13. In this context, the veil was used to demarcate class and status. In order to avoid mistaking a "free" woman for a slave, the latter were free to walk about the city uncovered, while free women on the other hand were veiled.

26. Michelle Hamilton, *Representing Others in Medieval Iberian Literature* (New York: Palgrave, 2007), 29.

27. See Marín, "Marriage and Sexuality in al-Andalus," 14.

28. As Leila Ahmed has pointed out, violent rivalry among harem women in different parts of the premodern Muslim world was not uncommon. Stories are told of women poisoning and consipirng to murder their rivals. *Women and Gender in Islam*, 84.

29. While these slaves' freedom and sensuality have been celebrated, the reality is that as slaves they were entirely at the mercy of their owners. There are stories of Andalusi slaves who lived in comfort and abundance in their masters' palace, but

there are also stories of abuse and cruelty toward slaves who refused to obey their owners. See Marín, "Marriage and Sexuality in al-Andalus," 14.

30. Ibid., 5.

31. Montaner, *Twisted Roots: Latin America's Living Past* (New York: Algora, 2003), 47–48.

32. Ibn Hazm, *The Ring of the Dove: A Treatise on the Art and Practice of Arab Love*, trans. A. J. Arberry (London: Luzac, 1953), 74.

33. John Gill, *Andalucía: A Cultural History* (New York: Oxford University Press, 2009), 100.

34. Gloria López de la Plaza, *Al-Andalus: Mujeres, Sociedad y Religión* (Málaga: Universidad de Málaga, 1992), 157–58.

35. Averroes, *Averroes on Plato's Republic*, trans. Ralph Lerner (Ithaca: Cornell University Press, 1974), 59.

36. Lebbadi, *Feminist Traditions in Andalusi-Moroccan Oral Narratives* (New York: Palgrave, 2009), 110.

37. Manji, *The Trouble with Islam*, 55.

38. James DenBoer, ed. "String of Pearls: Sixty-Four 'Romance' *kharjas* from Arabic and Hebrew *Muwashshahat* of the Eleventh-Thirteenth Centuries," *eHumanista* (Monographs in Humanities, 6), available at http://www.ucsb.edu/projects/ehumanista/projects (15 June 2012).

39. See Doris Earnshaw, *The Female Voice in Medieval Romance Lyric* (New York: Peter Lang Publishing, Inc., 1988), 33–37.

40. Using written material for pornographic purposes was not uncommon. Ibn Hazm tells the story of a man who masturbated using his lover's letter. Ibn Hazm, *The Ring of the Dove*, 72.

41. For more on jihad in Islam, see David Cook, *Martyrdom in Islam* (Cambridge: Cambridge University Press, 2007).

42. Shabbir Akhtar points to the euphemistic use in the Qur'an (24:60) of the term *qawa'id* (sitting ones) to refer to "older women past the prospect of marriage." Akhtar, *The Quran and the Secular Mind: A Philosophy of Islam* (New York: Routledge, 2008), 382 n.24.

43. It is important to point out that patriarchal concerns provoked by men's engagement in war are not specific to the Islamic context. For example, studies have shown that the two World Wars triggered in the U.S. fears over women's sexual agency and misogynist rumors about women's sexual deviance. See Susan Zeiger, *In Uncle Sam's Service: Women Workers with the American Expeditionary Force, 1917–1919* (Ithaca: Cornell University Press, 1999); and Leisa D. Meyer, *Creating GI Jane: Sexuality and Power in the Women's Army Corps During World War II* (New York: Columbia University Press, 1996).

44. In one of the most commented passages of the Qur'an husbands are given permission to physically punish women who persist in their transgression (4:34). The verb used in Arabic is *daraba* (to beat or to strike), though there are scholars who have attempted to attenuate the severity of the verse. See Bernard Lewis, *A Middle East Mosaic: Fragments of Life, Letters, and History* (New York: Random House, 2000), 185.

45. In his treatise, Ibn 'Abdun forbids women from occupying spaces that would give them access to men such as the river bank or the interior of a barber shop. For more on the regulations of women we well as other marginal groups in Muslim Seville such as Christians and Jews, see English translation by Bernard Lewis in Olivia Remie Constable, ed., *Medieval Iberia: Readings from Christian, Muslim and Jewish Sources* (Philadelphia: University of Pennsylvania Press, 1997), 175 – 79. However, Norman Roth warns against taking Ibn 'Abdun's regulations as a reflection of Andalusi reality. As he puts we: "we must not allow ourselves to be misled by such widely-publicized sources as the twelfth-century market regulations of Seville, written by Muhammad Ibn 'Abdun, which undoubtedly are more a reflection of the 'ideal' situation sought by a fanatical jurist than the actual situation in Seville [. . .]." Roth, *Jews, Visigoths and Muslims in Medieval Spain: Cooperation and Conflict* (Leiden: E. J. Brill, 1994), 114.

46. Ibn Hazm, *The Ring of the Dove*, 100.

47. DenBoer, "String of Pearls," n.p.

48. Translation found in Zwartjes, *Love Songs from Al-Andalus*, 214.

49. DenBoer, "String of Pearls," n.p.

50. "Encanto, encanto, entrad aquí / cuando el marido sea herido," found in Maria Jesus Rubiera Mata ed., *Poesía femenina hispanoárabe* (Madrid: Castalia, 1989), 47. I would like to thank Estela Harretche for her help with translation.

51. As Olivia Remie Constable has observed, there were different categories of merchants in al-Andalus, one of which is the *rakkad*, or those who travelled for trade. *Trade and Traders in Muslim Spain* (Cambridge: Cambridge University Press, 1994), 52–53.

52. Robinson, *Medieval Andalusian Courtly Culture in the Mediterranean: Hadith Bayad wa Riyad* (New York: Routledge, 2007), 113–114.

53. As María Jesús Viguera Molíns has pointed out, Arab chroniclers have used women for political propaganda. As she explains, "the enemies of the [Almoravid] dynasty, entrenched in pro-Almohad historiography, accused that empire of being perverted because they gave power to their women." Viguera Molíns, "A Borrowed Space: Andalusi and Maghribi Women in Chronicles," in *Writing the Feminine: Women in Arab Sources*, ed. Manuela Marín and Randi Deguilhem (New York: I.B. Tauris, 2002), 167. It would not be far-fetched to assume that the Almohad's ennemies, too, may have used depictions of women's transgressions of the social order to ridicule the Almohad and expose their weakness.

54. For more on *Hadith Bayad wa Riyad*'s context, see Robinson, *Medieval Andalusian Courtly Culture in the Mediterranean*, in particular "Alfonso, the Almohads and the 'Ajouz: The *Hadith Bayad wa Riyad*, Courtliness and Culture in Thirteenth-century Iberia," 113–70.

55. Robinson, *Medieval Andalusian Courtly Culture in the Mediterranean*, 26.

56. Fatima Mernissi, *The Veil and the Male Elite: A Feminist Interpretation of Women's Rights in Islam*, trans. Mary Jo Lakeland (Reading: Addison-Wesley Publishing Company, 1991), 92.

57. Ibid., 60–62.

58. Samar Habib, *Female Homosexuality in the Middle East: Histories and Representations* (New York: Routledge, 2009), 30–31.

59. The complete interview can be found at http://www.gauchemip.org/spip.php?article6545 (6 June 2012).

60. Abdelwahab Bouhdiba, *Sexuality in Islam*, trans. Alan Sheridan (London: Routledge & Kegan Paul, 1985), 113.

61. Ibid., 151.

62. Ksikes insists that "De grands auteurs comme Tifashi, Tijani, ou encore (et surtout) Nefzaoui étaient aussi de fervents admirateurs de la femme, pour laquelle ils avaient le plus grand respect et les plus délicates attentions." Driss Ksikes, "Erotisme: Quand les musulmans osaient," *TelQuel* 13 April 2006, available at http://www.telquel-online.com/219/couverture_219_1.shtml (6 June 2012).

63. Abdellah Tourabi, "Saphisme, homosexualité, plaisirs défendus: L'histoire insoupçonnée de l'érotisme en terre d'Islam," *TelQuel* 30 October 2010, available at http://www.telquel-online.com/445/images/Erotisme.pdf (6 June 2012)

64. Tariq Ali, *The Clash of Fundamentalisms: Crusades, Jihads and Modernity* (New York: Verso, 2002), 58.

65. Al-Nafzaoui, *The Perfumed Garden of the Cheikh Nefzaoui: A Manual of Arabian Erotology*, trans. Sir Richard F. Burton (New York: Signet Classics, 1999), 153–71.

66. Ibn Hazm, *The Dove's Neckring*, 22.

67. Ibid., 76.

68. As Appiah writes, "The real political question . . . [is] when we should endorse the ennobling lie . . . We . . . need to show not that . . . [these lies] are falsehoods but [that] they are useless falsehoods at best or—at worst—dangerous ones." Appiah, *In My Father's House*, 175, quoted in Eller, *The Myth of Matriarchal Prehistory: Why an Invented Past Won't Give Women a Future* (Boston: Beacon, 2000), n.p.

69. Ibid., 188.

70. Just in Casablanca alone, in addition to Lycée Ouallada, there is College Khnata bent Bekkar, named after a woman, Hinata (d. 1742), who supposedly ruled Morocco after the death of her husband Sultan Ismail Ibn Sharif (r. 1672–1729). There is also Lycée el Khansa, named after Tumadir bint 'Amir ibn al-Harith ibn 'Amr (575–644) known by her nickname al-Khansa, the famous seventh-century poet and contemporary of the Prophet Muhammad. According to medieval sources, she competed along with male poets with her poems, most of which were of elegy to her brothers Sakhr and Mu'awiyah who died in intertribal warfare.

71. Osama Bin Laden, *Messages to the World: The Statements of Osama Bin Laden,* ed. Bruce Lawrence, trans. James Howarth (New York: Verso, 2005), 14.

72. Clifford Krauss, "The Saturday Profile; An Unlikely Promoter of an Islamic Reformation," *New York Times* 4 October 2003, available at http://www.nytimes.com/2003/10/04/world/the-saturday-profile-an-unlikely-promoter-of-an-islamic-reformation.html (4 June 2012).

73. Moghissi, *Feminism and Islamic Fundamentalism: The Limits of Postmodern Analysis,* 17.

74. David William Foster, *Spanish Writers on Gay and Lesbian Themes: A Bio-critical Sourcebook* (Westport: Greenwood Press, 1999), 77.

75. For example, on January 22, 2000, university professor 'Aliya Shu'ayb, novelist Laila Othman, and their publisher Yahiya al-Rubay'an, were sentenced in Kuwait to prison for publishing what were considered "indecent" sexual writings. See details of the event in
http://www.ifex.org/kuwait/2000/01/25/writers_publisher_sentenced_to/ (6 June 2012).

76. The Qur'an, and to a great extent the *hadith,* condemn homosexuality. As a jurist, Ibn Hazm's views on homosexuality are necessarily shaped by both. It is not a surprise therefore that, in spite of his more positive accounts of homosexuals, he states in the chapter on "Of the vileness of sinning" that "As for conduct like that of the people of Lot, that is horrible and disgusting" *The Ring of the Dove,* 258.

TWO

Sex in Context

Western Representations and the Limits of Edward Said's Orientalism

When we think of Western representations of Muslim women it is hard not to think of Edward Said's influential work, *Orientalism*. More than three decades after its publication, it continues to be the reference *par excellence* in studies of the relationship between the West and the Muslim world. "Orientalism," according to Said, is "a style of thought based upon an ontological and epistemological distinction made between the 'Orient' and (most of the time) 'the Occident.'"[1] Said argues that Orientalists, a group comprised of women and men from a wide variety of disciplines, have produced a discourse about the Orient that is inaccurate and degrading.[2] This chapter seeks to complicate our understanding of Western representations of Muslim women in premodern French and Iberian literature. I argue that, by focusing on post-Enlightenment discourse, Said neglects a large corpus of European literature, which, at least until the seventeenth century, introduced more nuance into the West's understanding of Islam and Muslims than Said and the Saidian scholars acknowledge.[3] The first three sections of this chapter examine often-overlooked key French and Iberian texts from the thirteenth through the seventeenth centuries. These examples are meant to convey that, far from the idea that there has been only an isolated or recent interest in Islam on the part of the West, the two have a long, interconnected history. Moreover, we see that even in the premodern period itself, there is heterogeneity in perceptions of Muslim women, who are imagined not only as princesses but also as mothers, neighbors, lovers, and allies. The last section of this chapter turns to Said's *Orientalism* and what I argue are its proble-

matic legacies for the study of Muslim women. In addition to neglecting
the heterogeneity of Western literature about Muslim women, Saidian
scholars' double standard when dealing with the representation of Muslim women is motivated by an anti-Western rhetoric that ultimately silences criticism of misogyny in Muslim contexts.

MUSLIM WOMEN AND THE MEDIEVAL FRENCH IMAGINARY

Relatively little attention has been paid to medieval Western literature in
the debates about representations of Muslim women, in spite of the
wealth of information such literature provides.[4] One example can be
found in the late eleventh-century *Chanson de Roland*, one of the best-
known *chansons de geste*, or French epic poems.[5] The text is loosely based
on the historical Battle of Ronceveaux (778), in which the troops of
Charlemagne (742–814) fought against the Basques, except that in *Roland*
the enemy is the Muslim army. The poem tells the story of an attack by
Muslims as Charlemagne's army is withdrawing from Spain after a
seven-year campaign against Islam. Charlemagne puts his nephew, Roland, along with 20,000 men in the rear guard to protect the troops. Motivated by jealousy, Ganelon, Roland's father-in-law, betrays Charlemagne
and makes a deal with the Muslims, who attack the Christian army,
resulting in Roland's death. Charlemagne, informed of the tragedy, returns to defeat the Muslims, forces them to convert, and conquers the rest
of Spain.[6] Given the historical context—a time of conflict between Christians and Muslims—the author's portrayal of Bramimonde, a Muslim
woman, is especially interesting and one which complicates the para-
digms of Saidian ideology.

Throughout the poem, Muslims are depicted as both different and
similar. Although the author constructs Muslims as brutal and savage in
sections of the text—"Then they send him flying to the ground at their
feet / And beat him and smash him to pieces with huge sticks" (2587-88),
their characters also trigger admiration—"If only you had seen the
knights from Arabia, / the men of Occian, of Argoille and Bascle!"
(3473–3478). When the Muslim and Christian kings encounter one another in the battle they appear to be equal in strength and courage
(3560–78). Inspired by postcolonial theories, one might be quick to dismiss this binary representation as yet another example of the West's ambivalence about the Muslim man, who is viewed as both "familiar" and
"alien."[7] Such ambivalence, however, can also be explained in the context
of the text's genre. Although the epic is not concerned with historical or
even religious accuracy—for example, it confuses monotheist Muslims
with pagans—it does build on the familiar, a historical event and the
courtly Muslim, to introduce the grotesque and entertaining. As John
Victor Tolan puts it: "The goal of the poet here [in *Roland*] is the same as

that of the filmmaker portraying quintessential bad guys: to allow the reader (or viewer) to enjoy the violence, to revel in the blood and killing, without remorse. Only by dehumanizing the adversary, making him sufficiently 'other,' is this possible." At the same time, however, the Muslim man "cannot be made too other, for it is not valorous to slaughter mere beasts."[8] A critical reading of *Roland*, taking into account the typical characteristics of the epic genre, may be a more suitable method of analysis to explain such ambivalence.

Unlike her male coreligionists, the Muslim woman Bramimonde is spared the vilification relegated to her male counterparts. Rather than obstructing Christian victory, she functions as a mediator. The text describes a ceremony that involves Bramimonde, her husband King Marsile, and Ganelon (who plots against his coreligionists). Bramimonde offers Ganelon gifts to take to his wife:

Then Queen Bramimonde came forward:
'I love you dearly, lord,' she said to the count,
'For my lord and his men hold you in very high esteem.
I shall send your wife two necklaces,
Made of gold and full of amethysts and jacinths;
They are worth more than all the wealth in Rome.
Your emperor has never seen their like.'
He took them and pushed them into his boots. (634–41)

This scene shows the ease with which Bramimonde can communicate with Ganelon, highlighting her ability to understand and be understood without the need for a translator.[9] More importantly, the exchange introduces doubt about Bramimonde's allegiance. While the two men are solely preoccupied with their own immediate gain, Bramimonde evokes the absent woman, Ganelon's wife. It may be an exaggeration to suggest that Bramimonde has a feminist agenda, especially since she does not seem to care about the welfare of other women; the passage does, however, suggest that Bramimonde is not devoid of power and agency. She asserts her agency to voice her views, even if they go against other Muslims' beliefs, when she turns against her coreligionists, mocking their idols' helplessness when it comes to assisting her husband:

Bramimonde said: 'Now I hear great foolishness.
Those gods of ours have abandoned the fight;
At Rencesvals their powers deserted them;
They allowed our knights to be slain
And they let down my own lord in battle.
He has lost his right hand, he no longer has it;
Count Roland the powerful cut it off. (2714–20)

Bramimonde goes on to predict that the Christian emperor "will have the whole of Spain in his power" (2721). She even praises him in the presence of her husband: "The emperor is valiant and a fine warrior / he would sooner die than abandon the field. / No king on earth would regard him as a child. / Charles fears no man alive" (2737–40). Her harsh, insensitive words, as Kahf suggests, eventually prove fatal to her injured husband.[10] He dies, the poem tells us, of "grief" (3646–47). Bramimonde is one of the many women who have been neglected by Saidian scholars—a true rebel who uses her intelligence and agency to facilitate a dialogue between Christians and Muslims, and questions the sacredness of Islamic patriarchy.

Another woman character who introduces more nuances into Western representations of Muslim women is Nicolette in *Aucassin et Nicolette*, a thirteenth-century Old French romance written in verse and prose.[11] Nicolette enters the text having already converted from Islam to Christianity. She is the biological daughter of the Andalusi Muslim king of Cartagena. Kidnapped at an early age, she was sold to a French Christian viscount who baptized and raised her as his own. Her lover is Aucassin, whose father, the count of Beaucaire, objects to his son's relationship with Nicolette and imprisons him. Meanwhile, Nicolette escapes from the tower where the viscount has imprisoned her to prevent her from seeing her lover. Before taking refuge in a forest, she visits Aucassin in his underground cell, in a scene that emphasizes both his powerlessness and her ability to travel and cross boundaries at will. A series of events leads Nicolette to Cartagena, where she reunites with her brothers and father, the king, who tries to marry her to another Muslim king, but Nicolette refuses. She eventually manages to escape and finally rejoins her lover Aucassin. They marry and live happily ever after.

The thirteenth century in which *Aucassin et Nicolette* was produced marked a turning point in East-West and Muslim-Christian relations—in the East, the "Latin Empire" of Constantinople was established in 1204 after the Fourth Crusade's conquest of the Byzantine Empire, while in the West, the Christian Monarchs of Aragon, Castile, and Navarre defeated the Almohads in the battle of las Navas de Tolosa in 1212, marking the beginning of the end of Muslim political presence in Iberia. By the mid-thirteenth century, the Balearic Islands and most of Iberia had come under Christian rule, including the most important Andalusi cities, Cordoba, in 1236, and Seville, in 1248. At the same time, however, a sophisticated thirteenth-century trade network that connected the various regions of the Mediterranean and beyond, in a period that presents a challenge to Said's separate and categorical construction between East and West.[12] Nicolette's presence in Beaucaire reflects both the political and the economic circumstances of the thirteenth century: it is likely that she was captured as a result of a Muslim military defeat,[13] and, economically, Nicolette is a luxury commodity. As Jane Burns has suggested, the fact that she is acquired by the "very rich" viscount might be indicative of her high cost, not to mention the explicit references to her worth in gold.[14]

Such status might explain why the viscount has cherished her to the point of raising her as if she were his biological daughter.

Whether appreciated for her economic value or for her political significance [as a reminder of Christian defeat over Muslim kings], in Beaucaire Nicolette does not have any difficulty passing for a "true" French woman. She is repeatedly described as blonde, white, and pious. However, away from Beaucaire, Nicolette turns black. At one point in the text she disguises herself as a black *jongleur* in order to escape from her biological father's kingdom.[15] Yet before reuniting with her lover, Nicolette washes off and turns white again. Before making assumptions about medieval French society's fear of or unwillingness to accept a Muslim woman unless she "whitens" herself, it is important to take into consideration the religious context: in the thirteenth century, France, a nation that had yet to emerge and come into maturity, was dealing with other religious dissidents more threatening than Islam.

Aucassin et Nicolette was produced around the same time as one of the bloodiest events in French history, the Albigensian Crusade (1209–1229), which targeted "heretical" Cathars. Since the twelfth century, the Cathars had been gaining followers in the south of France, and by the early 1200s, they had become the dominant religion in Languedoc, making them more dangerous to Christianity than the Muslims.[16] Thus, unlike holy wars that targeted an external enemy, the Albigensian crusade was aimed at those within. In *Aucassin et Nicolette*, Nicolette's transformations outside Beaucaire recall some of the common beliefs about the Cathars more than they do her Muslim identity.[17] For example, Nicolette's strength and independence evoke some of the characteristics associated with Cathar women. Although recent historical scholarship has been skeptical of whether or not Cathars lived in a society that is egalitarian in terms of gender, the surviving documentation of the era suggests that Cathar women had more access to power than did their Catholic counterparts. Even inquisitorial studies show the important role that Cather women played as ministers, at times almost equal in number to men.[18] Moreover, Nicolette's healing abilities link her closely to Cathar women. When Aucassin falls in the forest, dislocating his shoulder, she heals him using plants.[19] Cathars, particularly women, were believed to have similar abilities. Testimonies from southern France in the first half of the thirteenth century report that Cathars traveled with the specific purpose of healing the sick.[20] If thirteenth-century readers picked up on these similarities, and they probably did given the seriousness with which the Cathar threat was taken, then what they would have feared more than Nicolette's Muslim origin was that she was possibly Cathar. This would also explain the reaction of Aucassin's father, who would have had more to lose if he were found to be associated with the Cathars.

To dismiss Nicolette as yet another example of Western misconstruction and misrepresentation of Muslim women is to ignore a complex context that reveals a more involved representation of Muslim women than a mere reflection of the West's conflictive relationship with Islam. These texts are rich enough to have challenged readers for centuries. They were composed in a context distant from ours, and yet they continue to inspire a variety of interpretations and fulfill an equally varied set of agendas, even today. Regardless of how one chooses to read them, this literature merits more than to be reduced to illustrations of the West's failure to understand Muslim women.

THE IBERIAN MUSLIM WOMAN CAUGHT IN AN INTIMATE CONFLICT

If a side-by-side study of Bramimonde and Nicolette exposes the many nuances one confronts when examining medieval French representations of Muslim women, such nuances are even greater in the Iberian context, for Muslims occupy an even more intimate place in Spanish history, making the representation of Muslim women both different and more complex. Muslims arrived in Iberia as early as 711, led by Tariq ibn Ziyad, and maintained a political presence until 1492, when the Nasirids, the last Muslim dynasty in Iberia, lost the kingdom of Granada. This history of Muslims in Spain not only complicates medieval Christian Iberian representations of Muslim women, but it complicates the terminology with which such representations can be discussed. Binaries such as East/West, Islam/West, Islam/Europe, Europe/Africa, or even North/South of the Mediterranean do not apply. In this period the West included Arabic-speaking Muslims, to whom western Europe is home and "origin," while African empires (the Almoravid and the Almohad) had a European capital (Seville). Thus, while Nicolette might be described in the French text as coming from "a foreign land," the Muslim woman in a Christian Iberian text from the thirteenth century is a native. As territories shifted from the rule of a Muslim king to a Christian one, Muslims that remained in newly Christian lands, known as *mudéjares*, continued to be active members of Iberian society while remaining Muslim. Such daily contact with Muslims explains why, contrary to French representations which focus mostly on the Muslim princess and aristocratic woman, Christian medieval Iberian literature depicts Muslim women from varied economic classes.

This is especially the case in the Galician-Portuguese collection of poetry and music *Cantigas de Santa Maria*, composed and compiled by King Alfonso X, "el Sabio" (the "Wise" or "Learned") (r. 1252–1284). *Cantiga* 167, for example, tells the story of a Muslim woman who, having heard from her Christian neighbors of miracles performed by the Virgin, decides, in the face of objections from her Muslim community, to make a pilgrimage to the Virgin's shrine in Salas to implore her to resuscitate her son who has been dead for three days. When the Virgin succeeds, the Muslim woman, who has witnessed the miracle with her own eyes, converts to Christianity. A refrain is repeated throughout the *cantiga* to emphasize the Virgin's inclusion: "The Virgin will aid whoever trusts in Her and prays faithfully to Her, *although he be a follower of another law*" (emphasis added).[21]

In *Cantiga* 205, Mary once again intervenes to help a Muslim woman in distress. The *cantiga* tells of the Christian siege of a Muslim castle on the frontier. A Muslim woman holding her child finds herself at the top of the burning tower. Appearing like the Virgin, she provokes the pity of Christians witnessing the scene, who pray on her behalf. The Virgin answers their prayers and saves the Muslim mother and her child. The Muslim woman converts to Christianity and her son is baptized. Once again, the *cantiga* proves that the Virgin answers not only the prayers of "good Christians," but those of all who love her and call for her help, regardless of their religion.

To understand such representations of Muslim women, it is important to contextualize. The collection of *Cantigas* was produced at a time of great political instability between Christians and Muslims. As Francisco Prado-Vilar has pointed out, it makes sense that Muslim women and their children are rescued and revived to be converted given Alfonso's preoccupation with the expansion of the Christian population in recently conquered territories.[22] However, such conversion and insertion into Christian society imply that the Iberia that Alfonso constructs in his *Cantigas* is not one that expels or excludes Muslims. Instead, it is one that is also nurtured by Muslim/Christian mothers.

Of course, not all Iberian representations of Muslim women are inclusive of Muslims. A case in point is the brief fifteenth-century *Romance de la morilla burlada* (Ballad of the Deceived Muslim Maiden), in which a young Muslim woman is tricked into opening her door to a Christian man who pretends to be a family member running for his life because he has just murdered a Christian man. Although the point is not stated, the audience is left to believe that the young Muslim woman is raped.[23] The *Morilla burlada* exposes the downside of intimacy. It is the product of a society in which a Christian's knowledge of Arabic is possible, and where such knowledge does not automatically raise suspicion about the man's religious identity. Moreover, the ballad describes a negotiation between a Muslim and Christian as it occurs in the same space (in Iberia), divided by a door. Ironically, it is ultimately the Christian man's intimate knowledge of Arabic and Islamic culture that enables him to deceive the *morilla*. In the *Morilla burlada*, the Muslim and Christian men are also alike in their patriarchal attitudes. If the Muslim woman is used in the war between Muslims and Christians, as Louise Mirrer insists in her study of the romance, then such war can only be possible when both sides value honor and virginity. In her construction of Muslims as the victims of

Christianity, Mirrer leaves out the fact that the importance the Muslim man attributes to honor and virginity makes him a conspirator in the rape of the Muslim woman. Far from being solely the victim of the Christian man, the *morilla*'s tragedy comes from her position between conflicting and oppressive patriarchies. As we will see in chapter 5, this complication for women does not end in the middle ages.

THE MUSLIM WOMAN IS NOT HERE, FOR NOW

By the second half of the sixteenth century, the intimacy between Islam and the Christian West becomes even more complex. The Christian man's words to the *morilla* would now have been a crime: edicts had made the use of Arabic in speaking and writing, as well as the possession of Arabic books, unlawful.[24] Muslim converts to Christianity came to be known as Moriscos (literally "little Moors"), and all efforts were made to exaggerate their difference from "legitimate" citizens and to construct these Iberian natives as aliens: inferior, greedy, untrustworthy, and dangerous.[25] Tension between Old Christians and Moriscos resulted in uprisings such as the Alpujarras revolt in Granada in 1568–1570. Old Christians grew even more untrusting of the Morisco population, fearing they might be aided by their coreligionists, the Turks, who were extending their power over much of the early modern Mediterranean.[26] Finally, between 1609 and 1614 as many as 300,000 Moriscos were expelled from the Iberian Peninsula.[27] The majority of these exiles settled in African cities in Morocco, Algeria, and Tunisia.

It is in this context of fear and political instability that Cervantes wrote "The Captive's Tale" (*Don Quijote* I. 39–42).[28] The tale's heroine, Zoraida, is a North African Muslim whose adoration of the Virgin Mary, we are told, has inspired her to embrace Christianity, adopt the name María, and move to Spain.[29] Her story is told by her travel companion, the Captive, a Christian soldier who had been imprisoned in Muslim territories, first in Constantinople, then in Algiers, where he met Zoraida. Thanks to the wealth of her father, Agi Morato, or Hajj Murad, Zoraida finances the escape of the Captive and his companions, on the condition that she accompany them to Spain. When she arrives at the Spanish inn where she and the Captive seek rest in the middle of their journey, Zoraida attracts the curiosity of the residents, even more than does her companion. In spite of his "Moorish" dress, there is no doubt that the Captive is a Christian. Zoraida's identity, on the other hand, causes confusion. Dorotea, one of the women in the inn, asks the Captive: "is this lady a Christian or a Moor? Her dress and her silence make us think that she is what we would rather she was not." To reassure his hosts, the tale's narrator, the Captive, insists that his companion is "Moor in her dress and body, but in her soul she is a devout Christian because she has a very strong desire to be one." Zoraida herself intervenes to confirm that she is indeed a Christian woman. When her companion refers to her as *Lela* (Lady) Zoraida, she strongly objects: "No! No Zoraida! María, María!" She then confirms "Yes, yes, María; Zoraida *macange*!" The reader is told that *macange* is "a word that means 'no'" (I.37).

In her analysis of Zoraida's answer, Mohja Kahf explains that *macange*, or "*ma kan chey* in Arabic means more than simply 'no' or 'not Zoraida at all'; it suggests that Zoraida never existed, that Zoraida has never been anything. It is a denial of history, echoing the Spanish state policies that have systematically made it seem as if the Moors had never existed, had never been in Spain at all."[30] Kahf's interpretation makes sense in the context of early modern Spain's national project to negate Iberia's Muslim heritage. It is even tempting to compare Zoraida to other Western representations of Muslim women who are stripped of their Muslim identity and brought into the West for the sole pleasure of the Western man, as in the case of early twentieth-century postcard photographs of partially nude Algerian women (discussed later in this chapter) that French colonialists used to send friends and family members back home. However, there are details in the text that raise questions about Zoraida's conversion. Even before her leaving Algiers, Zoraida's father casts doubt about the motives behind her conversion. As he explains to the Captive and his companions, his daughter's conversion and desire to travel disguise her yearning for sexual experience: "do not think she has been moved to change her religion because she believes yours is superior to ours, but only because she knows that in your country there is more lewd behavior than in ours." Rather than deny it, Zoraida simply states that it is a matter of perspective, and that what seems "wicked" to her father may appear "virtuous" to her (I.41). Zoraida herself invites readers to doubt her. In her own words, Muslims are "all false" (I.40) but Christians don't fare much better: they "always lie and pretend to be poor in order to deceive the Moors" (I.41). She repeatedly warns the Captive against trusting others, and doesn't even trust him herself. Despite his reassurances that he will marry her, she incessantly questions the Captive's intentions (I.40).

Even her understanding of Christianity raises suspicion about her conversion. In the letters through which Zoraida communicates with the Captive while still in Algiers, it appears that Zoraida's conversion is facilitated by her Islamic knowledge rather than a negation of her Muslim identity. As she explains:

> When I was a little girl, my father had a slave woman who taught me in my own language a Christian Zalá, or prayer, and she told me many things about Lela Marién. The Christian slave died, and I know that she did not go to the fire but to Allah, because afterward I saw her two times, and she told me to go to a Christian land to see Lela Marién, who loved me very much. (I.40)

Zoraida the Christian woman continues to refer to God as Allah. She refers to prayer as *zalá*, which comes from Arabic *al-salat*. As for Mary, she uses the term of respect *Lela* (*lalla*), which is still used today in North Africa, especially in Morocco. Zoraida's understanding of Christianity is therefore one that builds on and incorporates her Muslim heritage. It is a conversion that happens through what Paul Ricoeur refers to as "linguistic hospitality," a translation that rather than erase the specificity of the concept translated, retains it even while crossing the frontiers to another language.[31]

By becoming María, Cervantes' heroine thus does not necessarily cease to be Zoraida, since both identities are interconnected, at least linguistically. The linguistic elements also introduce nuance to her answer "No! No Zoraida! María, María! [. . .] Zoraida *macange*." While it is certainly plausible to read her response as a denial of her Muslim self, Zoraida's "no" can also be read as an affirmation of feminine voice and a rebellion against an existing paternalistic order.[32] The openness of Zoraida's first "no" (the fact that it is not followed by any specific signifier) could mean a denial of male authoritarianism, as she rejects the Captive's attempt to speak on her behalf, in itself a reaffirmation of the identity of Zoraida as a woman. Zoraida interrupts the Captive in his attempt to present her, and therefore himself, as a "true" Christian.[33] Why does Kahf interpret Zoraida's utterance as a denial of her subjectivity *tout court* instead of seeing it as a confirmation of her subjectivity *as a woman*? As a matter of fact, while the text's narrator tells us that *macange* means "no," Zoraida's answer invites an alternate interpretation if one considers the specificities of western Mediterranean African Arabic.[34] To the North African ear, "macange" sounds more like "makaynš(i),"[35] which is a combination of the negative "ma-š(i)" and "kayn," the active participle of *kun* (be), which means "to exist, to be present, there is/are."[36] "Ma-kayn(a)š" in the context of west North African Arabic means "is not here" or "there is not," thus connecting it to a specific time or place. It is still used today in places such as Morocco and Algeria when answering the telephone or the door to indicate that the person sought is not present, an absence that is meant to be only temporary. The answer is usually taken as an invitation to return or call again at another time. In order to avoid ambiguity, a simpler answer could have been used: "maši Zoraida" (it is not Zoraida) or "mani Zoraida" (I am not Zoraida). Moreover, there are ways in North African Arabic to communicate a "categorical negative" such as the omission of the suffix "š(i)."[37] Instead, Zoraida elects "macange," which, far from "erasing" her Muslim identity or indicating that she "never existed," simply communicates that Zoraida is not available *right now*, a temporary condition better conveyed with the Spanish *no está*.

Under the same hermeneutical principle, Zoraida's travel to Spain is a return of the already familiar Muslim to a Europe unsure about how to make sense of its heritage. This is best summarized in the reaction of the inn's residents to Zoraida's arrival. As if in denial when faced with a ghost, they ask if she is what they wish she were not, a Muslim. As it turns out, she is, among many other identities. Yet when she lifts her veil, her hosts forget the Muslim threat and succumb to her beauty:

> she lifted her veil and revealed a face so beautiful that Dorotea thought her more beautiful than Luscinda, and Luscinda thought her more beautiful than Dorotea, and everyone present realized that if any beauty could equal that of those two women, it was the Moorish lady's, and there were even some who thought hers superior in certain details. And since it is the prerogative and charm of beauty to win hearts and attract affection, everyone surrendered to the desire to serve and cherish the beautiful Moor. (I.37)

This recognition of Zoraida's beauty in the context of the beauty of Christian Iberian women (Dorotea and Luscinda), betrays the fragility of the walls of difference that early modern Iberian laws and edicts sought to erect between Christians and Muslims. Such appreciation is a reminder of how easily the Muslim woman fits in a society where, as Barbara Fuchs has pointed out, "Moorishness [. . .] is not only a historiographical relic but a vivid presence in quotidian Spanish culture."[38] When she lifts the veil, Zoraida, who was feared to be alien, is finally recognized as the same.

After all, how could a Muslim woman be alien to a society in which she has been present, visible, productive, and active for over eight centuries? It is undeniable that the early modern Spanish nation's relationship with Islam and Muslims was increasingly conflicted; however, Muslims, women and men, African, Arabs, and Amazighi, have been part of Iberia's identity and quotidian life for too many centuries to be simply erased. Such heritage does not solely manifest itself in Iberian architecture, food, and customs. Early modern Christian Iberians, like Iberians today, carry traces of their Muslim ancestors in their DNA. A recent study published in *The American Journal of Human Genetics* has identified high mean levels (10.6%) of North African ancestry in Iberians today, a fact that should not surprise any medievalist of the western Mediterranean.[39] It is perhaps this shared ancestry that Dorothea, Luscinda, and the inn's other residents recognize in Zoraida's face.

Cervantes subversively brings back to early modern Spain a Muslim/ Christian woman. However, rather than staging Islam and Christianity as opponents, Cervantes intelligently sketches a portrait of an immigrant who negotiates her double allegiances to both Islam and Christianity as she moves from one side of the Muslim Mediterranean to another, one that Muslims used to call home. Cervantes sheds light on his characters', and his own, multiple inheritances without which the history of Iberia, and Europe in general, cannot be understood, while at the same time, through his heroine, he represents an early form of religious hybridity that points to avenues of complicated cohabitation, but cohabitation nonetheless, between the then two dominant religions.

THE LIMITS OF *ORIENTALISM*

Taken together, the texts discussed so far reveal that Europe's literary landscape is populated by Muslim women such as Bramimonde, Nicolette, *la morilla*, and Zoraida. In examining these texts, I do not intend to invent a "Golden Age" of the West's relation with Islam, the age *before* imperialism and colonialism. As the analysis of these pre-colonial texts from the eleventh to the seventeenth centuries shows, Muslim women always fulfilled an ideological function. This fact, however, does not justify reducing a text to a mere reflection of the West's supposed intolerance of Islam. The women I have discussed in this chapter show that the West is heterogeneous in its portrayal of Muslim women, both geographically (in the sense that Spain's relationship with Islam and Muslim women is different from France's), and historically (the Muslim woman in the thirteenth-century *cantiga* fulfills a role different from the one played by a Muslim woman in the text of Cervantes in the seventeenth century). There is also heterogeneity in terms of class, a fact that is not highlighted enough in the scholarship about medieval representations of Muslim women. Not all Muslim women in medieval Western literature are imagined as princesses in need of rescue. There are princesses, but there are also women from different socioeconomic status. They may be honest, pious, liars, victims, criminals, manipulative, wealthy, and poor.

Yet all this heterogeneity has been erased from most discussions of representations of Muslim women, which have instead focused almost exclusively on how nineteenth- and twentieth-century Western writers, poets, painters, photographers, and travelers have misconstructed the Orient and its inhabitants. This reductive and simplistic view of the West's relationship with Muslim women is heavily influenced by Edward Said's *Orientalism*. In his book, Said describes Orientalism as "the corporate institution of dealing with the Orient—dealing with it by making statements about it, authorizing views of it, describing it, by teaching it, ruling over it: in short, Orientalism as a Western style for dominating, restructuring, and having authority over the Orient." Said views Orientalism not only as if affects the Orientals' "reality" but also, and more importantly, in terms of relations of power, insisting that "without examining Orientalism as a discourse one cannot possibly understand the enormously systematic discipline by which European culture was able to manage—even produce—the Orient politically, sociologically, militarily, ideologically, scientifically, and imaginatively during the post-Enlightenment period."[40]

Although Said himself has not paid much attention to the western Muslim Mediterranean, *Orientalism* has had a profound impact on the scholarship dedicated to the analysis of Western literature, paintings, photographs, and films depicting women from the Maghreb. For example, Said's work has influenced art historian Linda Nochlin's own analysis of European art. [41] The prominent Moroccan feminist Fatima Mernissi, whose writings are discussed extensively in the following chapter, was also inspired by Said's critique of Western representations of Muslims. This is particularly evident in one of her later works, *Scheherazade Goes West: Different Cultures, Different Harems* (2001), which I also address in the following chapter.

Another prominent scholar whose analysis of Western representations of Maghribi women is heavily influenced by Said's *Orientalism* is the Algerian academic Malek Alloula. In *The Colonial Harem*, Alloula criticizes what he calls Western "perversion," as evidenced by the postcard photographs of Algerian women that early twentieth-century French colonialists in Algeria sent to their friends and family back in France. Alloula argues that these postcards depict the harem as "a universe of generalized perversion and of the absolute limitlessness of pleasure." [42] However, it is not just the veracity of the photographers' accounts that is put into question. Alloula also questions the intent of these French Orientalists, whose postcards, he insists, are "an imaginary revenge upon what had been inaccessible until then: the world of Algerian women." [43] Women, in Alloula's discourse, are imagined as a locus of dispute between Western and Muslim men.

Hence, even though Said has been criticized by scholars such as Valerie Kennedy for his "almost total neglect of gender as a theoretical category," [44] he has nonetheless had an important impact on scholars working on issues of gender in the Middle East. [45] Yet in spite of its merits, Said's *Orientalism* has dangerous implications from a feminist standpoint. One of these implications is that rather than investigate complexity and nuance, *Orientalism*, as it has been interpreted by Saidian scholars, encourages simplistic statements about representations of Muslim women. Since it provides a simple and popular framework through which one gains a false sense of one's ability to navigate complex texts composed in different contexts, languages, and genres, *Orientalism* is often used as a facile formula through which students and scholars dismiss Western works as colonialist and imperialist, without permitting in-depth analysis.

This reductive approach often blinds readers to the critic's own patriarchal and misogynistic biases. As Winifred Woodhull has pointed out in her discussion of Alloula's *The Colonial Harem*:

> Implicitly, Alloula subscribes to the [. . .] view [. . .] that the affirmation of cultural traditions such as seclusion and veiling of women is necessary at a certain point in Algeria's history. But in suggesting this

without revision nearly twenty years after independence, Alloula repeats the gesture of the colonizer by making of the veiled woman the
screen on which he projects *his* fantasy [. . .]—that of an Algerian
nation untroubled by questions of women's oppression.[46]

In other words, what most concerns Alloula is not women's agency or
lack thereof, but rather the safeguarding of the patriarchal order by
which it is the Muslim man's desire and duty to keep the Muslim woman
veiled. The postcards reflect badly on Alloula, for they are bitter remin-
ders for him, and by extension for the Muslim man generally, of his
failure to keep "his" woman veiled and hidden away from the Western
man's gaze. Alloula thus exposes the androcentric nature of *Orientalism*,
for it appears that at the core of Said's work is a preoccupation all too
familiar in the Arabo-Muslim world since the Middle Ages, namely, *'ird*
or honor, as discussed in the previous chapter. What *Orientalism* conceals
under layers of sophisticated academic jargon is what has been practiced
and believed since the Middle Ages, that an attack on a Muslim woman's
honor is an attack on the man's, and that it is therefore his duty to defend
it, except that sword is now being replaced with a pen.

Orientalism is an extension of the patriarchal social order for, while
Muslim men's norms and rules seek to contain the physical bodies of
Muslim women, *Orientalism* maintains the same control over the representations of these bodies. Ironically, Alloula does not question his own
complicity in disseminating the photographs of these women by including them in his book.[47] Alloula would, however, undoubtedly have
found *his* representation of Muslim women different from a Western
man's; ultimately, the critique of Orientalist representations, at its core,
reflects a malaise related to *other* men representing *our* women. It is not so
much about *what* is said than about *who* says it. A case in point is the
literature discussed in the previous chapter. Most of Islam's celebrated
writers, poets, and theologians have written, at times extensively and
explicitly, about women's sexuality. Moreover, and contrary to what
Mernissi suggests in her discussion of Scheherazade, not all Westerners
who have written about Muslim women have imagined them in a harem,
as evident in the absence of the harem from the premodern texts discussed in earlier sections, and not all Muslim writers have privileged a
woman's intellect over her body. Take for example the following passage
from al-Nafzaoui's *The Perfumed Garden*:

> The kiss on the mouth, on the two cheeks, upon the neck, as well as the
> sucking up of flesh lips, are gifts of God, destined to provoke erection
> at the favourable moment. God also was it who has embellished the
> chest of the woman with breasts, has furnished her with a double chin,
> and has given brilliant colours to her cheeks.
> He has also gifted her with eyes that inspire love, and with eyelashes
> like polished blades.

He has furnished her with a round belly and a beautiful navel, and
with a majestic crupper; and all these wonders are borne up by the
thighs. It is between these latter that God has placed the arena of the
combat; when the same is provided with ample flesh, it resembles the
head of a lion. It is called the vulva. Oh! How many men's deaths lie at
her door? Amongst them how many heroes!
God has furnished this object with a mouth, a tongue, two lips; it is like
the impression of the hoof of the gazelle in the sands of the desert. [48]

A question calls out for answer here: Why is it that al-Nafzaoui's text, as
explicit as it is, is celebrated, even regarded as an indication of a time in
which Islam was "tolerant" (as discussed in the previous chapter), while
the text's nineteenth-century translator, Richard Burton, is ridiculed as
part of an imperialist agenda to dominate Muslims? [49] Why is it that al-
Nafzaoui, al-Tifashi, Abu Nuwas, and many others are praised for their
homoerotic literature, while Matisse's paintings of odalisques are dismissed as mere Orientalist fantasies of French colonialist dominance over
an inferior Muslim? [50] To further complicate matters, it is possible that
Matisse did indeed read al-Nafzaoui's *Perfumed Garden* and other texts
widely available in European translations, such as the *Thousand and One
Nights*, which would make his paintings a representation of a representation, rather than an attempt to represent and therefore "distort" the reality of these Muslim women? Why then is patriarchal anxiety an issue
only when it comes to Western representations, and not of their Muslim
counterparts? Why is the issue of "reality" raised only in the case of
Western writings, not Muslim texts? Are Western texts more deserving of
rigorous analysis than Muslim ones? Could it be that Western writers
and artists are ultimately held by Saidian scholars to higher standards
than are their Muslim counterparts? If the critique of representation is in
the context of colonial power relations, then why have Said and Saidians
not addressed Islam's own problematic representation of the *jahiliyya*, or
'asr al-jahiliyya (literally the "age of ignorance")? David Cook has questioned why, in Said's account and in postcolonial studies generally, imperialism is almost exclusively associated with the West, while in fact "Arab
Muslims have a long and well-documented imperialist and colonialist
past." [51] Islam's own foundational narrative, which remains largely un-
questioned by postcolonial theorists, came at the expense of a construction of Muslims' superiority vis-à-vis the *jahiliyya*. Why is it that Said and
Saidians have not questioned the Muslim-centric accounts of the *jahiliyya*
as an uncivilized era of barbaric practices and sexual promiscuity?

These questions are not meant to defend or excuse the patriarchal
motives behind Western representations. If anything, such questions
show that women, whether in medieval accounts or contemporary representations, are caught between conflicting patriarchies and that their
voices cannot figure in this discourse. However, these questions highlight
the double standard to which representations of Muslim women are sub-

mitted, depending on the critic. In other words, *Orientalism* reduces itself
to this: who has the moral claim over the Muslim woman and her body?
Muslim artists have the license to sexualize the Muslim woman's body,
whereas Western artists don't. Such double standards are taken to their
extreme in the work of the Moroccan-born, New-York based artist Lalla
Essaydi. Essaydi's work, as she insists, is "inspired" by Orientalists *and*
Edward Said. It is interesting to see how, while the "Orientalist" master-
pieces are denigrated because of their colonialist association, Essaydi's
representations of Muslim women are praised simply because she is a
Muslim woman representing Muslim women.[52] Such privileging of the
"native" merely reverses the supposed hierarchy of Western superiority.
In this new model, it is the "authentic" Muslim who is superior. This
discourse of assigning authenticity is dangerous because anybody's authority can thus be challenged based on a fluid concept of authenticity. Is
Essaydi, a relatively wealthy Muslim woman who has spent much of her
adult life outside her native Morocco, more authentic, and therefore more
deserving of respect than others?

What is arguably as *Orientalism*'s most problematic legacy is its silencing of critique of the Muslim world, and Muslim patriarchy in particular.
Postcolonial theorists, inspired by Said's *Orientalism*, have been critical of
what they regard as the Western construction of the Muslim woman as a
victim and the West's desire to "save" Muslim women from Muslim
men. While "saving" Muslim women has indeed been used to justify
political ends, it is harmful to Muslim women, not to mention simplistic,
to dismiss Western critique of Islamic patriarchy as a mere reproduction
of Orientalist bias. Critics have been particularly harsh when it comes to
Western women, who, because of their access to the interior of Muslim
women's spaces including harems, have written elaborate accounts of the
women therein. One example is Edith Wharton, who documented her
observations during a trip to colonial Morocco in September 1917. In her
narrative, Wharton does not hide her admiration of the French and the
colonists' "achievements" in Morocco. In fact, she does not hesitate to
remind her readers that she visits as the guest of General Hubert Lyau-
tey, resident general of French Morocco, of whom she is very fond and to
whom she dedicates the book. Wharton, however, does not hold the same
regard for Moroccan men and women. In Fez she describes her host and
the master of a harem as "a patriarchal personage, draped in fat as in a
toga." It is the women, however, who catch her attention:

> All the ladies of this dignified official household wore the same look of
> somewhat melancholy respectability. In their stuffy curtained apart-
> ment they were like cellar-grown flowers, pale, heavy, fuller but frailer
> than the garden sort. Their dresses, right but sober, the veils and di-
> adems put on in honour of my visit, had a dignified dowdiness in odd
> contrast to the frivolity of the Imperial harem. But what chiefly struck
> me was the apathy of the younger women. I asked them if they had a

garden and they shook their heads wistfully, saying that there were no gardens in Old Fez. The roof was therefore their only escape: a roof overlooking acres and acres of other roofs, and closed in by the naked fortified mountains which stand about Fez like prison-walls.[53]

Describing Wharton's account, Hermione Lee writes that Wharton "turns Morocco into a dream world [. . .], a fairy tale out of the Arabian Nights with *djinns* and magic carpets. She is fascinated by the sense of an unbroken line stretching back from this 'rich and stagnant civilization' to the times of the Romans. And, like all the French writers on Morocco, she finds there a sense of fatalism, apathy and somber melancholy."[54] When commenting on Wharton's "The Seed of Faith" (1919), Lee claims that the story "is full of the same kind of orientalist details as *In Morocco*."[55] Judith L. Sensibar evokes Said's writing about travel books: "Said points out that they, like other literary texts, function as 'a kind of intellectual *authority* over the Orient within Western culture'." She concludes that "Wharton's travel book 'represents' Orientalist 'truth'".[56] Similarly, Hasna Lebbady writes that "The view that Moroccan women [in *In Morocco*] are ignorant and passive, because they are supposedly harem-bound, derives from a predominantly Colonialist/Orientalist perspective."[57]

The concerns that Lee, Sensibar, and Lebbady have expressed about Wharton's praise of the French colonial government in Morocco are certainly valid.[58] However, they are so quick to dismiss her writing that they do not pause to think about Wharton's critique of the situation of the women she encountered in Morocco. What if women's oppression within the harem is in fact a reality, at least for some women, rather than Wharton's malicious colonial imperialist invention? After all, Morocco's most prominent feminist, Fatima Mernissi, wrote about her own experience growing up in a harem in Fez in the 1940s. Mernissi, too, wrote about the injustice of life in the harem, though, unlike Wharton, she also highlighted women's resistance in the harem, as discussed in the chapter 3. Moreover, the passage quoted above was not the first time in which Wharton expressed interest in women's welfare. She had already expressed her concerns on behalf of women, what one could describe as a feminist consciousness, in her other writings about women in other societies, including her own upper-class circle in Manhattan.[59]

Regardless of Wharton's true intentions and concerns, to dismiss out of hand her observations about the status of women in the harem is to miss an opportunity to criticize the patriarchal order in a society such as Morocco. Even today, comments about the status of Muslim women are faced with a violent response and the accusation of Orientalism. Western feminism itself is rejected under the pretext that it is "white," colonialist, imperialist. Such rejection of Western feminism is detrimental to the future of Muslim women. For, rather than build on a rich tradition of Western feminism, women are forced into an unhealthy and conflicted relationship with the West. Even when the critics themselves are Arab, Muslim, *and* women, they are accused of being Orientalists. A case in point is the Egyptian journalist Mona Eltahawi. In an article published in *Foreign Policy*, "Why do they Hate Us?" Eltahtawi exposes the patriarchy, abuse, and violence that women still endure in "post-revolutionary" Egypt, as discussed in chapter 5. Soon after its publication, commentators were quick to post on their blogs and Twitter feeds that Eltahtawi is an Orientalist who caters to the West's fantasies about Muslim women.[60] Similarly, the controversial writer Hirsi Ali and other critics who insist on the need for reform within the Muslim world are said to "share a common Orientalist heritage."[61] Iranian writer Azar Nafisi is, in the words of Hamid Dabashi, a "post-Orientalist."[62] It is especially troubling when Islamic feminists silence the critiques of other women masking their actions as a supposed resistance to the West. In a televised encounter between Eltahawi and Leila Ahmed, one of the most prominent Muslim feminists, Ahmed suggested that she understood Eltahawi's concerns but that it would not be wise to speak publicly about them, since doing so would fuel Islamophobia.[63] This rejection of criticism because it comes from the West, or rejecting criticism *tout court* under the name of Orientalism, is dangerous because it can stand between Muslim women and true reform. Muslim women must no longer be a taboo topic; the oppression and struggles of these women need to be expressed in novels, in poetry, in paintings, in ballet performances, in blog entries, in tweets, in political speeches; such oppression needs to be spoken aloud and *acknowledged*.

In this chapter I have argued that Said's *Orientalism* neglects a large body of premodern Western literature in order to construct an image of the West as anti-Islam, imperialist, and incapable of understanding or truly representing Muslims. I have complicated this notion by showing examples of Muslim women in foundational Western literature who are more than merely vulnerable, sensual objects of the Western man's desires and fantasies. In doing so, I do not seek to defend the West, nor do I claim that premodern literature lacked an ideological function; rather, I seek to interrupt and challenge automatic and simplistic associations between the West and representations of Muslim women that the popularity of Said's *Orientalism* has produced.

Additionally, in the same way that the previous chapter questions the "feminist utility" of the myth of al-Andalus, this chapter points to the harmful consequences of *Orientalism* for a feminist agenda concerned with Muslim women's progress. Such progress is hindered by *Orientalism*'s silencing of any criticism that refuses, in an effort to avoid fueling Islamophobia or anti-Arab sentiments, to paint Muslim women in an unproblematically positive way. Even though Said and the Saidian's objective for the most part is to question and deconstruct what they see as the binaries that Orientalists establish between the West and the Orient, through their protectionist discourse about Muslim women they end up ghettoizing Muslim women, inventing for them a world that is distinct from the one to which the West aspires. The dangers of this division between opposing arguments of what is appropriate for Muslim women will now become increasingly evident in chapter 3, which examines the limits of Islamic feminism through the work of Fatima Mernissi, one of the most influential feminist scholars of the Muslim world, and the most studied Moroccan scholar in the West. The chapter looks at the limits of Mernissi's hermeneutical focus on early Islamic texts, which confine women within the constraints of the sacred. In later studies, Mernissi resorts to a constructed Islamic "Golden Age," similar to the one discussed in the previous chapter, in order to cater to the populist post-9/11 discourse of "us" vs. the West, which ultimately takes precedence over feminist engagement.

NOTES

1. Edward Said, *Orientalism* (New York: Vintage Books, 1979), 2.

2. Said insists, "Anyone who teaches, writes about, or researches the Orient—and this applies whether the person is an anthropologist, sociologist, historian, or philologist—either in its specific of its general aspects, is an Orientalist, and what he or she does is Orientalism" (*Orientalism*, 2). The complicity of Orientalists with the colonialist agenda is an important thesis of Said's. As he puts it, "My contention is that Orientalism is fundamentally a political doctrine willed over the Orient because the Orient was weaker than the West, which elided the Orient's difference with its weakness." Ibid., 204. For an extensive critique of Said's Orientalism, see Ibn Warraq, *Defending the West: A Critique of Edward Said's Orientalism* (Amherst: Prometheus Books, 2007).

3. Medievalist scholars have pointed to Said's reductive and simplistic reading when it comes to medieval European literature. See Lisa Lampert-Weissig, *Medieval Literature and Postcolonial Studies* (Edinburgh: Edinburgh University Press, 2010).

4. For an extensive study of Western representations of Muslim women that includes the Middle Ages as well, see Mohja Kahf, *Western Representations of the Muslim Woman: From Termagant to Odalisque* (Austin: University of Texas Press, 1999).

5. All English references of the *Chanson de Roland* are to Glyn Burgess' translation. *The Song of Roland* (London: Penguin, 1990).

6. The identity of who attacked Charlemagne depends on the source. According to ninth-century chroniclers, it was the Basques who attacked Charlemagne's troops. According to thirteenth-century Arab chronicler Ibn al-Ahtir, it was Muslims from Saragossa. See Michael Routledge, "Songs," in *The Oxford Illustrated History of the Crusades*, ed. Jonathan Riley-Smith (Oxford: Oxford University Press, 1997), 91.

7. Said, *Orientalism*, 72.

8. John Victor Tolan, *Saracens: Islam in the Medieval European Imagination* (New York: Columbia University Press, 2002), 126.

9. Mohja Kahf has observed that Muslim women in medieval Western Christian texts do not appear to need translators when communicating with Christians. *Western Representations of the Muslim Woman: From Termagant to Odalisque*, 88.

10. Ibid., 23.

11. All English references of *Aucassin et Nicolette* are to *Aucassin et Nicolette and Other Tales*, trans. Pauline Matarasso (Harmondsworth: Penguin, 1971).

12. See Janet L. Abu-Lughod, *Before European Hegemony: The World System A.D. 1250–1350* (New York: Oxford University Press, 1989).

13. As Olivia Remie Constable has pointed out, Muslim slaves had been present in Christian European societies, including southern French cities, throughout the eleventh and twelfth centuries. In the thirteenth century, however, their presence "can often be directly linked to Christian victories in Islamic lands." Olivia Remie Constable, *Trade and Traders in Muslim Spain: The Commercial Realignment of the Iberian Peninsula, 900–1500* (Cambridge: Cambridge University Press, 1994), 234.

14. For more on Nicolette's worth in gold, see Jane Burns, *Sea of Silk: A Textile Geography of Women's Work in Medieval French Literature* (Philadelphia: U of Pennsylvania P, 2009), 127–28.

15. For a discussion of race this episode, see Jacqueline de Weever, *Sheba's Daughters: Whitening and Demonizing the Saracen Woman in Medieval French Epic* (New York: Garland, 1998), 26. Lynn Tarte Ramey on the other hand has argued that representations of Muslim heroines such as Nicolette "portray a period of questioning of the ability for two different peoples to coexist." Society, Ramey contends, "does not immediately accept these women. Only after a period of departure and a series of trials to prove their mettle can the Other come back and claim her place." Lynn Tarte Ramey, *Christian, Saracen and Genre in Medieval French Literature* (New York: Routledge, 2001), 93.

16. The Cathars' doctrine and way of life appealed to different economic classes. To most, they offered an appealing alternative from the corruption and brutality of the Catholic clergy as the "perfects," in addition to renouncing to luxury and worldly goods, were also against killing, including that of animals. To the Jewish and Muslim communities, the Cathars' belief in the goodness of all human souls offered a tolerant environment of cohabitation. See Gregory Stone, *Dante's Pluralism and the Islamic Philosophy of Religion* (New York: Palgrave Macmillan, 2006), 225–226. The doctrine also appealed to the rich and ruling elites, for the Cathars offered an opportunity to access some of the wealth accumulated by the church while at the same time they delivered them from the power of the local clergy. See Jill N. Claster, *The Medieval Experience, 300–1400* (New York: New York University Press, 1982), 337.

17. For a discussion of *Aucassin et Nicolette* in the context of the Albigensian Crusade, see Robert Griffin, "*Aucassin et Nicolette* and the Albigensian Crusade," *Modern Language Quarterly* 26 (1965): 243–56.

18. For more on the role of women in Catharism, see Anne Brenon, "The Voice of the Good Women: An Essay on the Pastoral and Sacerdotal Role of Women in the Cathar Church," in *Women Preachers and Prophets through Two Millennia of Christianity*, ed. Beverly Mayne Kienzle and Pamela J. Walker (Berkeley: University of California Press, 1998), 114–33.

19. "Running her hands over him, Nicolette found that his shoulder was dislocated. She manipulated and kneaded it so skillfully with her white hands [. . .] that it went back into its socket. Then taking flowers and fresh grass and green leaves, she made him a poultice with a strip of her shift, and he was completely healed" (XXVI, 10–14).

20. See Shulamith Shahar, *Women in a Medieval Heretical Sect: Agnes and Huguette the Waldensians* (Woodbridge: Boydell Press, 2001), 20.

21. All references to Alfonso's *Cantigas* in English come from the English translation, *Songs of Holy Mary of Alfonso X, The Wise: A Translation of the Cantigas de Santa Maria*, trans. Kathleen Kulp-Hill (Tempe: Arizona Center for Medieval and Renaissance Studies, 2000).

22. Francisco Prado-Vilar, "The Gothic Anamorphic Gaze: Regarding the Worth of Others," in *Under the Influence: Questioning the Comparative in Medieval Castile* (Leiden: Brill, 2005), 97.

23. See Louise Mirrer, *Women, Jews, and Muslims in the Texts of Reconquest Castile* (Ann Arbor: University of Michigan Press, 1996), 26–27.

24. Luce López-Baralt, *Islam in Spanish literature: from the Middle Ages to the Present.* trans. Andrew Hurley (Leiden: Brill, 1992), 171.

25. As Anwar Chejne puts it, "the Moriscos were singled out as a thorn in the side of the Spanish. Moriscan utterances, deeds, behavior, customs, dress, food, and very

manner of doing things were abominable and ought to be eradicated. Edict after edict was issued to correct or eliminate all features associated with Moriscos. As a people, they not only lacked purity of blood, but were crude and ignorant. They were often ridiculed as peasants, peddlers of figs, almonds, and other produce. Although they were considered industrious, hard working, thrifty, and family men, these virtues were read as competitive, greedy, avaricious, with a fecundity that would eventually upset the population balance. [. . .] In sum, he [the Morisco] was an undesirable stranger in his own land, denied the opportunity to adjust within the new religious order." Chejn, *Muslim Spain* (Minneapolis: University of Minnesota Press, 1974), 8.

26. In fact, faced with oppression and persecution by the Spanish Inquisition (1478–1834) in their homeland, the Moriscos appealed to both the Turks and Maghribis for assistance. See for example the anonymous Arabic poem c. 1501 in which the poet appeals to the Ottoman Emperor Bayazid II (r. 1481–1512) to intervene in Iberia on behalf of its Muslims. James Monroe, "A Curious Morisco Appeal to the Ottoman Empire," *Al-Andalus* 31(1966): 281–303.

27. Though the expulsion of the Morisco population had been proposed late in the reign of King Philip II (r. 1556–1598), it was enacted between 1609 and 1614, under Philip III (r. 1598–1621). Lu Ann Homza. "Introduction," in *The Spanish Inquisition, 1478–1614: An Anthology of Sources*, ed. Homza (Indianapolis: Hackett, 2006), xxxv.

28. All English references of the *Quijote* are to Grossman's translation. Miguel de Cervantes Saavedra, Miguel de. *Don Quijote*. Ed. and trans. Edith Grossman (New York: Harper Collins, 2005).

29. Even though this essay refers to Muslims and Christians as different categories, the reality of the early modern Western Mediterranean is more complex. For example, the historical Hajj Murad, Zoraida's father, was the son of a Christian woman slave. His wife, the mother of the historical Zoraida, was also the daughter of a Christian woman slave. María Antonia Garcés, *Cervantes in Algiers: A Captive's Tale* (Nashville: Vanderbilt University Press, 2002), 209.

30. Mohja Kahf, *Western Representation of the Muslim Woman: From Termagant to Odalisque* (Austin: University of Texas Press, 1999), 85.

31. Paul Ricoeur, *On Translation*, trans. Eileen Brennan (New York: Routledge, 2006), 10.

32. For example, Algerian feminist writer Assia Djebar sees in Zoraida a renegade who leaves the comfort of her father's home to seek the unknown: "Elle troque un espace cerné (la maison la plus riche d'Alger où elle était reine) pour un ailleurs illimité mais incertain." Djebar, *Vaste est la prison* (Paris: Albin Michel, 1995), 168.

33. As María Antonia Garcés has noted, "[f]ormulating the Algerian woman's identity within a Christian framework [. . .] is crucial for the former captive, for his own status as a Christian would be contested by his experiences in Barbary." Garcés, *Cervantes in Algiers: A Captive's Tale*, 211.

34. That is not to suggest that the Arabic spoken throughout the medieval and early modern western Mediterranean was uniform. Scholars such as G. Colin refer to a "bloc linguistique," which, in the pre-twelfth century, included Iberia, the Maghreb, Malta, and Sicily. Jeffrey Heath disagrees, though he concedes that the urban dialects of the Maghreb shared many similar features because of the exchange between the different Maghribi communities. Jeffrey Heath, *Jewish and Muslim Dialects of Moroccan Arabic* (New York: Routledge, 2002), 4–5.

35. The suffix "ši" is still used in Algerian as well as Moroccan Arabic, particularly in northern Morocco and in the Jebli dialect spoken in the region of the Rif Mountains.

36. Jeffrey Heath, *Jewish and Muslim Dialects of Moroccan Arabic* (New York: Routledge, 2002), 6.

37. Kristen Brustad, *The Syntax of Spoken Arabic: A Comprehensive Study of Moroccan, Egyptian, Syrian, and Kuwaiti Dialects* (Washington: Georgetown University Press, 2000), 306. It is impossible to determine with certainty the extent of Cervantes' knowledge of Arabic. However, judging from his use of western Mediterranean Arabic in his texts, and given his own encounters with Maghribi and Morisco Arabic in both Spain

and Algiers, it is safe to conclude that the author knew enough to distinguish between "makaynši" and "maši" or "mani." For more on Cervantes and Arabic, see Gamal Abdel-Karim, "La evidencia islámica en la obra de Cervantes: análisis y valoración," in *De Cervantes y el Islam*, ed. Nuria Martínez de Castilla Muñoz and Rodolfo Gil Benumeya Grimau (Madrid: Sociedad Estatal de Conmemoraciones Culturales, 2006), 41–57.

38. Barbara Fuchs, *Exotic Nation: Maurophilia and the Construction of Early Modern Spain* (Philadelphia: University of Philadelphia Press, 2009), 5.

39. Interestingly, the study shows that the highest portions of North African ancestry are not found in Andalusia, but rather in Galicia and Northwest Castile. Susan M Adams, et al., "The Genetic Legacy of Religious Diversity and Intolerance: Paternal Lineages of Christians, Jews, and Muslims in the Iberian Peninsula," *The American Journal of Human Genetics* 83 (December 2008): 725–736.

40. Said, *Orientalism*, 3.

41. See Linda Nochlin, "The Imaginary Orient," *Art in America* (May 1983): 118–131; 187–191.

42. Malek Alloula, *The Colonial Harem*, trans. Myrna Godzich and Wlad Godzich (Minneapolis: University of Minnesota Press, 1986), 95.
Paul Ricoeur, *On Translation*, trans. Eileen Brennan (New York: Routledge, 2006),

43. Ibid., 122. Writing about Turkish representations, Meyda Yegenoglu also sees Muslim women as a mere pretext, for the Westerner's desire for the Oriental "is always mediated by his desire to have access to the space of its woman, to the body of its woman and to the truth of its woman." Yegenoglu, *Colonial Fantasies: Towards a Feminist Reading of Orientalism* (Cambridge: Cambridge UP, 1998), 48.

44. Valerie Kennedy, *Edward Said: A Critical Introduction* (Cambridge: Polity Press, 2000), 12.

45. See Lila Abu Lughud, "Orientalism and Middle East Feminist Studies," *Feminist Studies* 27, 1(2001): 101–13.

46. Winifred Woodhull, *Transfigurations of the Maghreb: Feminism, Decolonization, and Literatures* (Minneapolis: University of Minnesota Press, 1993), 45.

47. According to Marnia Lazeg "Alloula dug up the colonial pictorial archives and 'violated' Algerian women once more by making titillating pictures available to a wider audience than the original." *The Eloquence of Silence* (New York: Routledge, 1994), 191.
190. Similarly, Carol Schloss criticized Alloula for exposing the women of the postcards: "If Algerian women were vulnerable and disgraced by their original display on colonial postcards, they are once again exposed by their display in this book." "Algeria, Conquered by Postcard," *New York Times Book Review*, 11 January 1987: 24.

48. Al-Nafzaoui, *The Perfumed Garden of the Cheikh Nefzaoui: A Manual of Arabian Erotology*. Trans. Sir Richard F. Burton (New York: Signet Classics, 1999), 12.

49. Rana Kabbani criticizes Burton for constructing Muslim women as "convenient chattels who offered sexual gratification." *Europe's Myths of Orient* (London: McMillan, 1986), 7.

50. See Marilyn Lincoln Board, "Constructing Myths and Ideologies in Matisse's Odalisques." *Genders* 5(Summer 1989): 21–49. On representations of homosexuality, see Joseph A. Massad, *Desiring Arabs* (Chicago: University of Chicago Press, 2006).

51. David Cook, "The Muslim Man's Burden: Muslim Intellectuals Confront their Imperialist Past," in *Postcolonial Theory and the Arab-Israeli Conflict*, eds. Donna Robinson Divine and Philip Carl Salzman (New York: Routledge, 2008), 129.

52. For more on Essaydi's work see Imani Cheers, "Q&A: Lalla Essaydi Challenges Muslim, Gender Stereotype at Museum of African Art," available at http://www.pbs.org/newshour/art/blog/2012/05/revisions.html (25 June 2012) Essaydi's official website is http://lallaessaydi.com/ (25 June 2012).

53. Edith Wharton, *In Morocco* (New York: Charles Scribner's Sons, 1920. Reprint. Hopewell: Ecco Press, 1996), 192.

54. Hermione Lee, *Edith Wharton* (London: Vintage, 2007), 517.

55. Ibid., 641

56. Judith L. Sensibar, "Edith Wharton as Propagandist and Novelist," in A *Forward Glance: New Essays on Edith Wharton*, ed. Clare Cloquitt, Susan Goodman, and Candace Waid (Newark: U of Delaware P, 1999), 160.

57. Hasna Lebbady, *Feminist Traditions in Andalusi-Moroccan Oral Narratives* (Basingstoke: Palgrave MacMillan, 2009), 81.

58. See Sharon L. Dean, *Constance Fenimore Woolson and Edith Wharton: Perspectives on Landscape and Art* (Knoxville: University of Tennessee Press, 2002), 43.

59. For a discussion of Western feminists' complex perception of the "Orient" see Charlotte Weber, "Unveiling Scheherazade: Feminist Orientalism in the International Alliance of Women, 1911–1950," *Feminist Studies*, 27.1(2001): 125–57.

60. See for example the following blog entry, http://frustratedarab.com/2012/04/24/us-and-them/.

61. Andrew Shryock ed., *Islamophobia/Islamophilia: Beyond the Politics of Enemy and Friend* (Bloomington: Indiana University Press, 2010), 13.

62. See Hamid Dabashi, *Post-Orientalism: Knowledge and Power in Time of Terror* (New Brunswick: Transaction Brooks, 2008).

63. The exchange can be viewed at the following link: http://www.youtube.com/watch?v=9Z0DB2XOoHc (25 June 2012).

THREE

Sacred Limits

Islamic Feminism, or Feminism Confined

In the preceding chapters, I examined the dangerous implications of Saidian critique and the myth of al-Andalus for Muslim women and the study of their representations. This chapter questions Islamic feminism and the compatibility of feminism with Islamic beliefs and practices. Islamic feminists argue that a return to a "true," "authentic" Islam will lead to justice for women. As Miriam Cooke has pointed out, rather than reject Islam, the Qur'an and the *hadith*, Islamic feminists work "within the systems that are trying to marginalize them" in order to challenge the patriarchy.[1] This chapter focuses on three strategies that Islamic feminists employ in order to achieve this work from within. One strategy consists of reinterpreting scripture from a feminist perspective to recover Islam's egalitarian message, which, it is argued, was lost in the male scholars' misogynistic interpretations of the Qur'an and the *hadith*. The second strategy is to make visible and celebrate Muslim women's resistance from within Islam and Islamic institutions. Often embracing cultural relativism at the expense of universalist values, these feminists return to what are often assumed to be oppressive institutions such as the veil and the harem in order to demonstrate the specifics of an Islamic context: one that Western feminist scholars presumably cannot understand to the same extent. Most of the Islamic feminist scholarship produced in the West falls into this category. The third strategy is to divert critique from Islam to Western culture. Rather than focus on Islamic patriarchy and the injustice that Muslim women endure within predominantly Muslim societies, these Islamic feminists focus on a struggle against the West. Such a shift in priorities produces at times a discourse that, in its zeal to defend Islam against the West, ends up defending injustice against women.

The goal of this chapter is to build on and develop these strategies of Islamic feminism as seen through the work of Fatima Mernissi, one of the most influential feminist scholars of the Muslim world. Her work on women and Islam has received much praise and her books have been translated into several languages. This chapter examines the limits of the strategies used by Islamic feminism through the discussion of three of Mernissi's most popular books: *The Veil and the Male Elite* (1991), *Dreams of Trespass* (1994), and *Scheherazade Goes West* (2001). I argue that, whether she focuses on reinterpreting Islamic texts, celebrating Muslim women's resistance, or critiquing the West, Mernissi's reliance on Islamic feminist strategies undermines a larger feminist agenda that is genuinely conducive to justice and significant social change for women.

ISLAMIC FEMINISM AND THE LIMITS OF HERMENEUTIC READINGS

In *Le harem politique: le prophète et les femmes* (1987), translated into English as *The Veil and the Male Elite: A Feminist Interpretation of Women's Rights in Islam* (1991), Mernissi writes:

> Clearly, the imams were able to take advantage of our ignorance of the sacred texts to weave a *hijab*—a screen—to hide the mosque/dwelling. But everyone knows that, as the Koran tells us "of use is the reminder," and all we have to do is pore over the yellowed pages of our history to bring to life 'A'isha's laughter, Umm Salama's fiery challenges, and to be present to hear their political demands in a fabulous Muslim city— Medina open to the heavens.[2]

Mernissi's argument in this passage, and throughout her book, is a common one repeated by Muslims, non-scholars and scholars alike: that at the level of the text (the Qur'an) Islam is progressive for women, much more so than were pre-Islamic Arab societies. This belief is at the core of Islamic feminism. Neither the Qur'an nor the Prophet is responsible for Islam's misogyny. Mernissi faults the male elite that undertook the task of transmitting the Prophet's sayings and practices, and of explaining the Qur'an. She argues that the members of the Arabian male elites inherited their sexist views from pre-Islamic customs, which Mernissi believes the Prophet Muhammad would have adamantly opposed. "Is it possible," she asks, "that Islam's message had only a limited and superficial effect on deeply superstitious seventh-century Arabs who failed to integrate its novel approaches to the world and to women? Is it possible that the *hijab*, the attempt to veil women, that is claimed today to be basic to Muslim identity, is nothing but the expression of the persistence of the pre-Islamic mentality, the *jahiliyya* mentality that Islam was supposed to annihilate?"[3]

To answer these questions, Mernissi returns to the "origin" of Islam in order to contrast its message with the misogynist, patriarchal order that existed before the revelation of the Qur'an, known as *'asr al-jahiliyya*, literally the "era of ignorance."[4] Islamic scholars often cite ways in which the welfare of women improved under Islam. For example, female infanticide, a practice that was supposedly common among Arabs, is forbidden in Islam. Islam also forbids the pre-Islamic practice of passing a wife as an inheritance to the heir of her husband upon the latter's death. Instead, Islam secures for women their own share of inheritance. The details of such inheritance, as Mernissi has pointed out, are spelled out in numerous Qur'anic verses.[5] By contrasting the ways in which Islam is better for women than the "age of ignorance," Mernissi and other Islamic feminists position their religion as a source of liberation.

Beyond highlighting the Qur'an's feminist message, Mernissi's agenda in *The Veil and the Male Elite* is to make sense of the *hadith*'s misogyny. She explains that Islam's "feminist" message met resistance from the Prophet's Companions, who sought to maintain the patriarchal order that existed among Arabs in the *jahiliyya*. Mernissi dedicates several chapters to a critique of the Prophet's Companions, in particular Abu Bakra and Abu Huraira. Men such as these have played a crucial role in the interpretation and transmission of the Prophet's sayings and teachings, yet they are rarely read critically, especially from a Sunni perspective.[6] One such saying is the *hadith* that was supposedly heard by Abu Bakra and recorded by al-Bukhari, according to which the Prophet said: "Those who entrust their affairs to a woman will never know prosperity." Unlike al-Bukhari, who assumes the *hadith* to be *sahih*, or authentic, Mernissi engages in an exercise of deconstruction. She examines, as she puts it, "where, when, why, and to whom" the *hadith* was uttered. She explains that Abu Bakra recalled the words of the Prophet twenty-five years after his death, in the context of a political conflict between Aisha, the Prophet's wife, and Ali, the cousin of the Prophet and the fourth caliph, who retook the Iraqi city of Basra after defeating Aisha in the Battle of the Camel. As a notable in Basra, Abu Bakra found himself in the uncomfortable position of having one side against the other. Mernissi argues that Abu Bakra opportunistically remembers the *hadith* to avoid declaring openly his allegiance to either. She also states that in one of his biographies it is recorded that Abu Bakra was flogged for false testimony in a case of *zina* (i.e., for illicit sexual act). Having discredited his intentions in uttering this *hadith*, Mernissi also introduces doubt about Abu Bakra as a source of *hadith* more generally. She concludes that Abu Bakra cannot be regarded as a reliable transmitter of *hadith*.[7]

Mernissi employs the same method to criticize the misogyny of one of the most important and prolific narrators of *hadith*, Abu Hurayra. She elaborates on his name as well as on his conflicts with the Prophet's wives. Originally from the Yemeni tribe in the region of Daws, 'Abd al-

Shams (Servant of the Sun), as he had previously been named, did not convert to Islam until the age of thirty. "Abu Hurayra," literally the father of the little female cat, is a nickname the Prophet gave him because he used to carry a cat. Abu Hurayra, however, objected to the feminine reference in his name, insisting that the nickname the Prophet gave him was "Abu Hirr" (father of a male cat). Such a dislike for the feminine, Mernissi comments, is ironic given that rather than engage in commercial or military activities, Abu Hurayra preferred to remain in the company of the Prophet, serving him and even "help[ing] out in the women's apartments."[8] What was seen as Abu Huraryra's "laziness" brought him into conflict with one of Muhammad's most powerful and feared Companions, 'Umar Ibn al-Khattab, who "disliked lazy people" and even offered Abu Hurayra a job, which the latter refused.[9]

Abu Hurayra also had a conflictive relationship with the Prophet's wives, in particular Aisha, who often challenged his understanding of Muhammad's words: "Father of the Little Cat, the next time you undertake to repeat the words of the Prophet, watch out what you recount." On another occasion when Aisha accused Abu Hurayra of reporting a *hadith* he had never heard, he responded "O Mother, all I did was collect *hadith*, while you were too busy with kohl and your mirror."[10] Although these anecdotes may seem trivial, they involve some of the most revered figures of Islam. Mernissi uses the canonical texts of Islam to uncover less commonly known stories about Muhammad's entourage and expose how words and practices falsely assigned to the Prophet by some of his Companions were used to reinforce the patriarchal and misogynist order that existed in the Arabian Peninsula before Islam.

In the second part of her book, Mernissi moves beyond the *hadith* and undertakes the even more challenging task of refuting traditional interpretations of the Qur'an. She focuses on women's veiling, beginning by contextualizing the verse about the *hijab*, which orders men to address the Prophet's women from behind a curtain. Mernissi examines the details surrounding the "descent" of the verse of the *hijab* through an anecdote narrated by another one of his Companions, Anas Ibn Malik, and recorded by al-Tabari, considered an authority in *tafsir* (explanation) of the Qur'an. The story takes place on the night of Muhammad's wedding with Zaynab Bint Jahsh. When the celebration was over, all the guests left except for three "who seemed oblivious of their surroundings. They were still there in the room, chatting away." The Prophet was presumably "annoyed" because he wanted to be alone with Zaynab, who is described as "a woman of great beauty." At some point, the Prophet Muhammad decided to leave the room to visit with his other wives in their apartments. Upon his return to Zaynab's room, the three guests were still there, chatting. Muhammad, who "was an extremely polite and reserved man," returned to Aisha's room. When he was finally informed of the guests' departure, Muhammad "came back to the nuptial chamber. He put one foot in the room and kept the other outside. It was in this position that he let fall a *sitr* (curtain) between himself and me, and the verse of the *hijab* descended at that moment."[11] Thus, the concept of a curtain, later a veil, is introduced, but as a separation between two men at the door of a woman's private chamber.

Through this story, Mernissi demonstrates that according to its *asbab al-nuzul* (the causes of the revelation) the verse of the *hijab* fulfills the social function of teaching etiquette to men. The *hijab* in this context has nothing to do with hiding a woman's body or suppressing its sexuality. If anything, the *hijab* is meant to facilitate the sexual union between the Prophet and his new wife, a union that is delayed because of the presence of the guests who refuse to leave. Moreover, in the story the Prophet does not find it problematic or worrisome to leave his beautiful new bride alone and unveiled with men who are not related to her.

In addition to this social function, Mernissi argues that the *hijab* had other functions, none of which aimed at concealing Muslim women's bodies. For example, in one instance in the Qur'an, the *hijab* in its metaphorical sense is used to signify the separation between two conflicting ideologies: the monotheism of Islam and the polytheism of the Quraysh tribe. The "veiled" polytheists are incapable of grasping the message of Islam. In this case, Mernissi argues, the *hijab* is considered as "something that diminishes human intelligence." In another instance, she quotes a medieval theologian who evokes the *hijab* as a punishment.[12] Finally, Mernissi herself points to the irony of how the *hijab* went from a "beginning" when it "had such a strong negative connotation in the Koran" and it was the "very sign of the person who is damned, excluded from the privileges and spiritual grace" to being something that has "claimed our day as a symbol of Muslim identity, manna for the Muslim woman." [13]

Through her feminist re-reading of canonical sources, the same ones used by scholars of Islam to marginalize women in public spaces, Mernissi distances what she constructs as "true" Islam and the Prophet's "original" message from the misogynist practices of Muslim men. However, this kind of approach is eventually, inevitably, confronted with writings that are unambiguously misogynistic, rendering these claims a desperate attempt at defending a text against its own message. Mernissi herself is aware of the limits of her defense, for she strategically avoids issues that could challenge her argument. For example, although she elaborates on the context of the descent of the verse of the *hijab*, she does not mention the verse often used by Islamic scholars to call for women's covering: In the Sura *al-Nur*, women are asked to cover their bosom with a *khimar*, or head cover.[14] Mernissi historicizes and contextualizes the earlier verse about the veil, yet she does not address this one, which evokes the veil in the context of the feminine body in public space, therefore making it more relevant from a feminist perspective. Moreover, it is not coincidental that Mernissi, like many other Islamic feminists, focuses mostly on the *hadith* instead of the Qur'an. As Hammed Shahidian puts it, "dismissal of some *hadiths* seems the easiest strategy, since unlike the Koran, which is considered to be the word of Allah, *hadiths* are merely stories from the prophet and the Imams, narrated by mortal human beings."[15] In other words, Mernissi has less to lose by criticizing Abu Huraira than if she were to criticize the Qur'an.

This selective approach is particularly evident when she addresses Mohammed's relationship with women. She constructs Islam as an accomplice in early Muslim women's transgressions against an Arabian patriarchy. In addition to Aisha, who constantly confronted and corrected Abu Huraira, Mernissi dedicates an entire chapter to "The Prophet and Women" in which she complicates Muhammad's approach to gender and sexuality. She insists, as is well known among Muslims and often repeated, that Muhammad's first wife, Khadija, was a powerful and wealthy entrepreneur who "asked for the hand of the Prophet." At the time of their marriage, Khadija was fifteen years older than Muhammad, who was then 25. Another of his wives, Umm Salama, came from a prominent Qurayshi family. She is known in Islamic sources for her inquisitive mind, which is why the Prophet discussed religious and political matters with her.[16] A verse about gender equality was written in response to a question she posed to the Prophet about the Qur'an's silencing of women.[17] Rather than dismiss Umm Salama's concerns, Muhammad addresses them in the public space of the mosque. More important, however, the anecdote implies that earlier verses of the Qur'an are imperfect in their exclusion of the feminine. Umm Salama's complaint was therefore necessary to complete Allah's message as mediated by the voice of Muhammad. Other women followed in Umm Salama's footsteps, visiting the Prophet to voice complaints about their status in the patriarchal Arabian society or to request that new laws be applied.

In *The Veil and the Male Elite*, therefore, Muhammad emerges as a man who is not only constantly surrounded by women—in the period on which Mernissi focuses, Muhammad was married to nine women—but who also values women's opinions and takes their advice. He is even constructed as a revolutionary heretic who sides with women against the Arabian male elite and their patriarchal values. At the same time, however, Mernissi purposefully omits issues that could problematize her argument. For example, she does not address the controversial issue of Aisha's age when the Prophet married her and how ultra-orthodox Muslims use it as a basis for establishing nine as a permissible marrying age for girls. Moreover, although Mernissi refers to Zaynab in the context of marriage to Mohammed, she neglects to mention that Zaynab was the wife of the Prophet's adopted son. The latter divorced her before Mohammed could marry her.

Mernissi further stresses Muhammad's revolutionary characteristics by creating a rupture between the time before Islam, the *jahiliyya*, and the era that followed. While pre-Islamic societies were also patriarchal, women in the *jahiliyya* were capable of attaining power.[18] Khadija, the Prophet's first wife, is a prime example. She was a successful businesswoman before she married Muhammad and before converting to Islam. Leila Ahmed has argued that what Muslims celebrate in Khadija, namely, "Her economic independence; her marriage overture, apparently without a male guardian to act as intermediary; her marriage to a man many years younger than herself; and her monogamous marriage all reflect *jahiliyya* rather than Islamic practice."[19] Ahmed contrasts the liberties that Khadija enjoyed as a woman who spent most of her life before Islam with the situation of Aisha, Muhammad's youngest wife, who was born to Muslim parents and married Muhammad when she was nine years old. Unlike Khadija, Aisha had to wear the veil and live in relative seclusion with the rest of the Prophet's wives. Nevertheless, as Ahmed explains, Aisha was still living in a moment of transition from the *jahiliyya*, and therefore enjoyed some of the opportunities available for aristocratic women in the *jahiliyya*: "Her brief assumption of political leadership after Muhammad's death doubtless had its roots in the customs of her forebears, as did the esteem and authority the community granted her. The acceptance of women as participants in and authorities on the central affairs of the community steadily declined in the ensuing Islamic period."[20] This decline in status and power explains why aristocratic women such as Hind Bint 'Utba, whom Mernissi mentions in the context of a controversial cannibalistic event—she supposedly ate the liver of the Prophet's uncle Hamza—were reluctant to embrace Islam.[21] Muslim society was therefore no less patriarchal than the societies that preceded it; from the perspective of women of the upper class, who had previously enjoyed a measure of independence, it was more so.

These silences in Mernissi's work are not the result of misinformation, since she addresses some of them in her earlier writings.[22] However, silences are telling, for they expose the limits that a critic confronts when constraining her readings within religious boundaries; and Mernissi is far from being alone. Inevitably, all Islamic feminists have to face a problematic passage of which they need to make sense. For example, in her book *Qur'an and Woman*, the prominent North American Islamic feminist Amina Wadud had to address the verse 4:34, one of the most commented verses on women. While the verse clearly instructs husbands to punish disobedient women by "striking" or "beating" them (*'idribuhunna*), Wadud argues that the Qur'an could not encourage violence against women and therefore the obedience required of women is to God not to the husband.[23] Moreover, Wadud attempts to find a way out of the controversy by proposing new meanings for "*daraba*," the root of "*'idribuhunna*." She explains that it does not "necessarily indicate force or violence" but can also mean to leave or to set an example.[24] Sadly, these elaborate explanations do not help the many women who are beaten in various parts of the world, the name of religious authenticity.

Needless to say, the intellectual work that Mernissi, Wadud, and other scholars do is important. It interjects the feminine voice in a field that seeks to silence it. Unfortunately, in spite of the best intentions of Islamic feminists, no matter the interpretations, contextualization, and at times acrobatic and selective readings, the reality is that there are texts and practices that are not compatible with feminism. In the process, Islamic feminists give the false impression that all that needs to be done to achieve justice is to reinterpret scriptures. In reality, there is much more that needs to be done in Muslim societies to achieve even a semblance of gender equality. Historically, women have never benefited from calls for return to "origin," "purity," and "authenticity," and Islamic feminism is no exception.

THE LIMITS OF MERNISSI'S CRITIQUE OF "LIMITS"

Unlike *The Veil and the Male Elite*, in which she focuses on the "official" textual Islam, *Dreams of Trespass* returns to Mernissi's personal experience growing up in a harem. In this autobiographical text, narrated in the voice of a child, Mernissi recounts her life and that of other women in her father's harem in Fez in the 1940s. However, as in *The Veil and the Male Elite*, Mernissi shifts the blame from "true" Islam, which, she argues, is an ally for women, to the ways in which men employ Islam in order to limit women's freedom and potential. *Dreams of Trespass* is an exploration of limits, or *hudud*. Mernissi examines how traditions and erroneous interpretations of Islamic texts are used to confine women in order to maintain patriarchal order in her father's harem. Much of the text however, is dedicated to recounting the ways in which women resist and transgress the *hudud*.

Hudud, the plural of *hadd*, literally means "limits" or "boundaries." It is the term used in religious texts to refer to the limits of acceptable behavior in an Islamic society. According to Islamic penal law, or *sharia*, *hudud* is one of the three major categories of crime. It covers offenses such as apostasy, drinking alcohol, illicit sexual relations, defamation (such as a false accusation of adultery), theft, and rebellion (such as the intentional attempt to overthrow a legitimate leader of an Islamic state).[25] A violation of the *Hudud* is considered a crime against God, and is therefore punished severely and cruelly. In *Dreams of Trespass*, *hudud* refers specifically to the limits that patriarchy imposes on women. On the text's first page, the narrator alerts her readers to the importance of *hudud*, explaining that, according to her father, harmony comes from respect of limits, especially those between women and men. Such harmony, in the Mernissi household, is maintained through the harem, an institution that guarantees the physical separation of women from men, though the limits in *Dreams of Trespass* are not just physical. There are also the *hudud* that draw the boundaries of women's critical thinking. For example, when the narrator's cousin, Malika, suggests that perhaps "a man needs a big thing under his *djellaba* to create a harem" and that maybe Ahmed, the harem's doorman, "has only a small one," her male cousin, Samir, intervenes to "put an end to that line of inquiry," after which the narrator was forced to restrict her "questioning to the *halal*, or the permissible." [26] While a child may be scolded for such talk, the reader can detect the limited intellectual space, between the *halal* and the *hudud*, within which the children, and adult women, must learn to remain confined.

The patriarchal status quo in the harem, Mernissi argues, is not only preserved by men dominating women, but also by women being complicit in their own oppression. For example, Lalla Mani, the narrator's paternal grandmother, is the one who maintains patriarchal order even in the absence of men. She is presented as a woman who has already paid her dues to the patriarchal society. She was a daughter, a wife, a mother, and now is an older woman who no longer is perceived as a sexual being, and therefore ceases to be a threat to the patriarchal order. She transforms herself into the patriarchy's eye inside the harem, vigilant of the details of women's quotidian activities to make sure that traditions are respected. She constantly mingles in the affairs of the younger women to make sure that the *hudud* are respected, often relying on the Qur'an, the *hadith*, and ancestorstral tradition for legitimacy. When women in the harem break too many tea glasses as they watch and perform plays inspired by the life of the famous Egyptian singer Asmahan, Lalla Mani declares theater a "sinful activity" since "it is not mentioned in the Koran, and no one ever heard about it in either Mecca or Medina." But, she adds, "if careless women still insist on indulging in theater, so be it. Allah will make everyone pay for their sins on Judgement Day. But breaking my son's tea glasses just because Asmahan, that scandalous lazybones is getting married, is utter recklessness." [27] Lalla Mani also doubts the religious validity of a picnic, which "might even be counted as a sin on Judgment Day." [28] She wants to keep everything she has inherited from her ancestors unchanged, including fashion, embroidery, and cooking. [29]

In *Dreams of Trespass*, Lalla Mani fulfills a function similar to that of Mohammed's Companions in *The Veil and the Male Elite*: just like Abu Hurayra and Abu Bakra, Lalla Mani, too, manipulates Islam, even trivializes its message, in order to maintain the existing patriarchal social order. This separation of Islam's true message from its corruption by self-invested individuals such as the Companions and Lalla Mani allows Mernissi to make sense of injustice against women without ever interrogating either the Qur'an or the Prophet. "True" Islam is always absolved of any blame. God in *Dreams of Trespass*, just like the Prophet in *The Veil and the Male Elite*, is also on the side of women. He is called upon by all kinds of transgressive women including the *Thousand and One Night* heroine Princess Budur who passes for a man and marries Princess Hayat al-Nufus.[30] He is "generous and gives every one of his creatures some beautiful thing, tucking it right inside, like a mysterious flower, without you even knowing it."[31] He is *latif* (sensitive) and *rahim* (forgiving). He "made Islam's territory immense and wonderfully diverse," thereby increasing the pool of potential Muslim husbands for the narrator and her cousin Chama.[32] He is responsible for the sex of the child, thus taking away the blame from the mother if she fails to produce a man.[33] He is called upon to make sure that two babies born the same day have the same celebration rituals regardless of their sex.[34] In her literary world, Mernissi introduces a feminized version of Islam that assists women in their subversions and against patriarchy.

Mernissi shares this desire to forge a space for the feminine within Islam with the most renowned Muslim feminists. Egyptian scholar Nawal El Saadawi writes about the Islam she learned from her grandmother:

> I learnt my first lessons in philosophy, my first lessons in religion and politics, from my grandmother. She had not read the book of God, had not been to school, but I heard her say to the village headman as she waved her big rough hand in front of his face: "We are not slaves and Allah is justice. People have come to know that through reason."[35]

The Islam that Saadawi and Mernissi describe is the one that Leila Ahmed calls "women's Islam," a spoken Islam different from the "official textual Islam" from which men claim their authority. Ahmed explains,

> there are two quite different Islams, an Islam that is in some sense a woman's Islam and an official, textual Islam, a "men's" Islam. And indeed it is obvious that a far greater gulf must separate men's and women's ways of knowing, and the different ways in which men and women understand religion, in the segregated societies of the Middle East than in other societies.[36]

Ahmed argues that "particular backgrounds and subcultures give their own flavors and inflections and ways of seeing to their understanding of religion," insisting that "there are not just two or three different kinds of Islam but many, many different ways of understanding being a Muslim." More importantly, Ahmed contends that women's Islam, which is also the Islam of "ordinary folks," is not "the Islam of sheikhs, ayatollahs, mullahs, and clerics. The Islam that women hear and speak is the "ethical" Islam, which is more concerned with justice and equality than with jurisprudence, which is at the center of "legalistic" Islam.[37]

In *Dreams of Trespass*, the child narrator voices a similar understanding of multiple Islams: "Throughout my childhood I had a very ambivalent relationship with the Koran. It was taught to us in a Koranic school in a particularly ferocious manner. But to my childish mind only the highly fanciful Islam of my illiterate grandmother, Lalla Yasmina, opened the door for me to a poetic religion."[38] This vision of an ethical Islam is particularly appealing to marginalized women, such as Aunt Habiba, who has been let down by men's legalistic Islam. While the father and Lalla Mani evoke *hudud* to delimit women's boundaries, to Habiba, who cried for years after she "had been cast off and sent away suddenly for no reason by a husband she loved dearly," Allah's *hudud* are the boundaries imposed on men to protect women not to subjugate them: "When you hurt a woman, you are violating Allah's sacred frontier. It is unlawful to hurt the weak."[39] According to Habiba, it is the imams, not Allah, who are to blame for the veiling of the woman's body.[40] She believes it to be her duty to question the imams and other patriarchs, for she thinks that *'aql* (reason) is the "the most precious gift" bestowed by Allah upon humans, with which one must question and speak back to authority.[41]

Having identified clearly the target of her critique, namely patriarchy and not the true words of Allah and his Prophet, Mernissi tells of how women such as Habiba and Chama, the "high priestesses of imagination,"[42] transgressed authority through storytelling. As soon as the other women finish their daily chores, they rush to the terrace or top floors, the spaces seldom visited by adult men, to hear Habiba's stories and watch Chama's plays. As far as Habiba is concerned, telling stories is in itself an act of resistance. As she reminds the other women, her husband took all her belongings, but he was unable to take away her "laughter and all the wonderful stories [she] can tell when the audience is worth it."[43] It is therefore not surprising that often the protagonist of her stories is Scheherazade, who used storytelling to avoid execution by a man.

Nevertheless, one is left wondering if what Mernissi posits as resistance is truly resistance or if it is simply a way for women to make sense of a condition imposed on them and from which there is no escape. After all, as Lebbady has pointed out, "dreams are very much in conformity with what patriarchy thinks women should be or do, as dreaming remains a perfectly ineffective form of trespass."[44] Unfortunately, rather than pursue this line of questioning, Lebbady merely dismisses Mernissi's narrative as resembling Orientalist tales in their exoticising of the harem.[45] Mernissi's exaggerated celebration of resistance in *Dreams of Trespass*, as in her other texts, is a consequence of the limits within which she frames her feminist critique. There will always be texts, practices, and conditions that Mernissi will fail to question since she adamantly refuses to cross the boundary of the sacred. Like her child narrator, Mernissi, too, confines her critical thinking within the boundaries of the religiously permissible.

The same critique can be extended to what Ahmed and Saadawi qualify as resistance. One should not belittle women's survival struggles, but, realistically, what can women do from a position of weakness other than appeal for divine intervention? Did Saadawi expect her grandmother to accuse the village headman openly and directly of being unjust? One is

left wondering if Mernissi's and other Islamic feminists' critique ultimately legitimizes already existing limits. Mernissi's refusal to interrogate norms is especially surprising given her choice of narrator. As a
child, the narrator is supposed to get away with asking questions that
adults are not willing to pose, since children supposedly do not have the
same social filters as adults. And yet the child in *Dreams of Trespass* seems
exaggeratedly preoccupied with finding that which ought to be celebrated in the harem such as her grandmother Yasmina's rebellion, Aunt Habiba's stories, her mother's nontraditional embroidery and beauty reci-
pes. The child narrator shares with Mernissi the same determination to
legitimize the true religious message by distancing it from patriarchal
misogynistic traditions. However, such distinctions, whether they are
gender-based (women vs. men) or truth-based (an "authentic" Islam vs.
falsehoods attributed to Islam) ultimately end up contributing to an apologetic discourse that further reinforces women's subordination. It is even
more problematic, not to mention perverse, when the women who have
suffered the most are made to defend the same institutions that have
oppressed them. It is understandable that Aunt Habiba may find psycho-
logical relief in her defense of a feminine form of Islam, yet the fact
remains that her husband, like many husbands in predominantly Muslim
societies, will continue to find the law on his side when it comes to
divorce.

MERNISSI GOES AGAINST THE WEST

Scheherazade Goes West: Different Cultures, Different Harems marks an important shift in Mernissi's critique as she turns her attention to the West
as the object of her analysis. Whereas in *The Veil and the Male Elite* and
Dreams of Trespass it is patriarchal misunderstanding of "true" Islam that
is at the core of Muslim women's oppression, in *Scheherazade Goes West* it
is the West that Mernissi blames for misconstructing Muslim women as
the oppressed victim of Muslim patriarchy. She writes, "In the 1920s,
when Matisse was painting Turkish women as harem slaves, Kemal Ata-
turk was promulgating feminist laws that granted Turkish women the
right to education, the right to vote, and the right to hold public office."[46]
To a great extent, it, too, is an autobiographical account constructed as a
reflection on and an answer to the questions and observations of the
Western men she encountered while on a book tour. As she writes: "During that tour, I was interviewed by more than a hundred Western journalists and I soon noticed that most of the men grinned when pronounc-
ing the word 'harem.' I felt shocked by their grins. How can anyone smile
when invoking a word synonymous with prison, I wondered."[47] Mernissi explains that in the West the harem "lost its dangerous edge."[48] While
in Arabic, the word "harem" derives from *haram*, or forbidden by relig-

ious law,[49] in the Western imagination it was transformed into a space of sexual excess.

In line with Edward Said's thesis in *Orientalism*, Mernissi came to find out that Western men's harem has nothing to do with the "real" harem. Western men's harems were an "orgiastic feast" where men received "sexual pleasure without resistance or trouble from the women they had reduced to slaves." In Muslim harems, on the other hand, "men expected their enslaved women to fight back ferociously and abort their schemes for pleasure." Moreover, while Westerners' knowledge of harems came from films, paintings, operas, and ballet performances by Ingres, Matisse, Delacroix, Picasso, Verdi, and Diaghilev, Mernissi's "harem was associated with a historical reality." The harems she "visualized [were] actual places—harems built of high walls and real stones by powerful men such as caliphs, sultans, and rich merchants."[50]

Even Muslim representations of harems, Mernissi insists, are radically different from their Western counterparts. Far from being silenced and submissive sexual commodities, Muslim women in Muslim men's representations are "much more realistic" in the sense that "Muslim men expect women to be highly aware of the inequality inherent in the harem system and therefore unlikely to enthusiastically satisfy their captors' desires."[51] Muslim men are aware of women's intelligence, therefore "even the most fervent extremists never argue that women are inferior, and Muslim women are raised with a strong sense of equality."[52] To illustrate her point, Mernissi returns to medieval representations in which Muslim writers and artists depict strong, rebelling Muslim women capable of crossing forests and rivers in pursuit of their lovers. She refers to the example of the romance of "Khusraw and Shirin" by the poet Nizami (1140–1209).[53] The story tells of the love between Shirin, the niece of the Queen of Armenia, and Khusraw, the son the Persian king Hurmuzd. After falling in love with Khusraw's portraits, Shirin jumps on a horse and leaves her aunt's kingdom in search of the prince. The manuscript consists of a series of brightly colored miniature paintings of Shirin that depict her riding her horse and hunting.[54]

Mernissi recalls those miniatures of Shirin while standing in the Louvre in front of Jean-Auguste Ingres' *La Grande Odalisque*, which illustrates a naked concubine looking over her shoulder with a sultry expression. Mernissi "could not help but laugh out loud" as she imagined an encounter between Shirin and Ingres:

> Would he have stripped her of her arrows and horse in order to paint her? Would he have taken away her silk caftan and clothes as well? And what about Immanuel Kant, who said knowledge kills a woman's charm, so that an educated woman might as well have a beard? At the thought of a fake beard under Shirin's lovely chin, I started laughing so merrily that the elegant French security guard on the Louvre's solemn and dark first floor, where *La Grande Odalisque* is imprisoned forever,

asked me to either chuckle more quietly or leave at once. I chose the second option and headed toward the rue de Rivoli exit, with my head up.[55]

Such mixture of the anecdotal and analytical has made Mernissi's writing approachable and has contributed to its popularity particularly in the West, where *Scheherazade Goes West* has become a classic feminist text. However, in her zeal to defend Islam and Muslims against the West and Western constructions, Mernissi is obliged to be selective in dealing with both Western and Muslim sources. For example, when she evokes medieval representations of Muslim women, such as the tale of Shirin and Khusraw, which she counters with Matisse and others, it would have made more sense for Mernissi to examine Christian medieval representations such as those discussed in chapter 2. Shirin is closer in her depiction to Nicolette from the thirteenth-century tale of *Aucassin et Nicolette* than she is to Ingres' odalisque. Both Shirin and Nicolette are physically strong and independent women capable of riding horses and crossing forests alone.

Moreover, Mernissi's constant need to "go East" to seek examples of the Muslim world rather than look at stories from the Muslim western Mediterranean betrays assumptions about a constructed "origin" and locus of authenticity associated not only with a time far off in the past, but also with a geographic space. A reliance on models from the western region of the Mediterranean, however, runs the risk of complicating Mernissi's project. A case in point is her discussion of the difference between Christian and Muslim views of baths. Rather than investigate the wealth of medieval Western literature and culture in its complex relationship with Islam, Mernissi justifies her ideology by using the Christian "dark" Middle Ages and stereotypes such as medieval Christians' poor hygiene. Westerners, she explains, associated bathing with disease and infection. She juxtaposes this "phobic attitude toward the baths" to eleventh-century Baghdad, which counted 60,000 public baths. Furthermore, according to Mernissi, "From the start, Christianity condemned bathing as a lustful sin." However, such "connection between the public baths and promiscuity is totally absent in Muslim culture, where, from the beginning, the strict separation of the sexes was the rule." [56] If Mernissi were to include eleventh-century Cordoba in her discussion, she would have found "Muslim" baths built by the Romans. Were she to read Muslim medieval scholars from the western Mediterranean, she would have found writing about sexual encounters in baths. In *The Perfumed Garden*, al-Nafzawi discourages both men and women from engaging in intercourse in the bath because it may be harmful to their health since "the water penetrating into the sexual parts of man or woman may lead to grave results." [57] The fact that al-Nafzawi warns against having intercourse in the bath suggests that such an act was not unheard of. It also suggests that the association between the bath and possible infection was not exclusively Christian and that, instead, it had to do with medieval medical theories shared by Muslims and Christians alike.

Furthermore, Mernissi equates separation of the sexes with absence of sexual desire, thus ruling out the possibility of homosexuality. Medieval Muslim writers tell a different story. In the thirteenth-century *Delights of Hearts, or What You Will Not Find in Any Book*, al-Tifashi includes anecdotes about men setting up rendezvous with one another at public baths.[58] In one case, a prominent man from Cairo who was not open about his homosexuality used the bathhouse as a "discreet" place to have sex with other men:

> he was a closet queen and a model of discretion in his behavior. He used to go to a certain public bath, where he had a private room always reserved for him. As soon as he arrived, the attendants who worked in the place would come running at his call and would go to give him personalized service. Naturally they too had to take all their clothes off so that he could look them over at his leisure. When he saw a cock he liked, he would signal to its proud owner, and the boy would gladly accede to his wishes. He kept these activities a secret and was especially careful not to use anybody as a go-between in his sexual transaction. Only employees of the bathhouse could testify as to what he really did and liked, but there were a lot of boys working there who had taken turns with him, so everybody knew what he was up to. Since he was so rich and gave the boys who serviced him generous tips, all the well-hung young hustlers and ne'er-do-wells were eager to become attendants at the bathhouse he used to frequent.[59]

As the examples from al-Nafzaoui and al-Tifashi show, and contrary to Mernissi's assumptions, the connection between the public baths and sexual relations was not "totally absent in Muslim culture." This association has survived even today in the jokes told throughout the Muslim world, though such jokes are often homophobic. In the controversial Egyptian film, *Hammam al-Malatily* (The Bathhouse of Malatily), the public bath is imagined as a space that allows for homosexual practices.[60] Though such art and rhetoric in Muslim societies are not uncommon, Mernissi silences even the possibility of homoerotic desire in the bath. Commenting on Ingres' depiction of two women erotically caressing each other in a bath, Mernissi writes that such a scene "would be impossible in a Moroccan *hammam* for the simple reason that it is a public space, often overrun with dozens of noisy children."[61] Speaking on behalf of all Muslim women, Mernissi writes that "we Muslim women don't rush to baths to look at our neighbors, and I myself don't like to stare too much at who is sitting near me because I am likely to encounter a colleague from the university or one of my students or the wife of my building's janitor."[62] Mernissi is capable of imagining the *hammam* as a space that brings together women of different socio-economic backgrounds, yet she cannot imagine such women as lesbians. This malaise with the homoerotic betrays the limits of Mernissi's intersectional critique. Trying to establish some form of authority for Islam over the West and Christianity, Mernissi selectively chooses her sources and thus ends up stripping Christians as well as Muslims, of their plurality.

This reductive discourse is particularly evident in the book's concluding chapter, in which Mernissi silences the heterogeneity of women both in the West and in the Muslim world. Even though *Scheherazade Goes West* rarely discusses Western women, Mernissi redirects her focus to these women whom she sees as the victims of the "size 6," which she labels "the Western women's harem." This chapter has been particularly popular among readers in the West. Mernissi argues that Western women are faced with restrictive standards of beauty that celebrate the slim youthful body. She recounts her experience in an upscale department store in New York City where a saleswoman informed her that there were no skirts her size because she was "too big." When asked who decides that a "size 6" is the norm for a woman's body, the salesperson replies, "It's all over, in the magazines, on television, in the ads. You can't escape it. There is Calvin Klein, Ralph Lauren, Gianni Versace, Giorgio Armani, Mario Valentino, Salvatorre Ferragamo, Christian Dior, Yves Saint-Laurent, Christian Lacroix, and Jean-Paul Gaultier. Big department stores go by the norm." If these labels were to cater to Mernissi's size 14 or 16, the salesperson insists, then "they would go bankrupt." Mernissi confesses that the experience in the store made her feel "savagely attacked" and that she lost her "usual self-confidence."[63]

Mernissi's lament about the fashion industry's confinement of the woman's body echoes the argument of another popular book, *The Beauty Myth* by Naomi Wolf, whom Mernissi quotes in her chapter. In *The Beauty Myth*, Wolf argues that the beauty industry has established unattainable standards of beauty in order to confine women's bodies. However, Mernissi, the salesperson, and Wolf all dismiss the role of women, who, in reality, far from being passive consumers, directly influence the beauty industry to accommodate various shapes and sizes. In fact, luxury brands such as Chanel have been selling plus-sized clothing because it is what their clientele has demanded. As a fashion commentator puts it: "These [high-end] labels have been producing plus-sized garments for years. Could you imagine if Valentino, Armani, Carolina Herrera, Escada, Donna Karan and Max Mara didn't make 12s, or 14s, or 16s? They'd be dunzo; those charity-gala-ladies-who-lunch-museum-board-members-who-'winter'-and-'summer' make up a big chunk of their markets."[64] This is not to say that "size" no longer matters in the fashion industry, nor do I mean to dismiss the voices of women who feel that they do not fit their society's beauty standards. However, when dealing with "the American woman" or "the Western woman" in the singular, Mernissi reduces Western women's experiences to a story of obsession with physical beauty and slimness. This is particularly ironic because she has dedicated much of her work to fighting the West's supposed fixed image of the submissive Muslim woman, yet she reduces American women to victims of size based on one singular experience she had in a department store in Manhattan.

Furthermore, in this exchange, Mernissi appears to be oblivious to the question of class.[65] She writes about Western women as if they were a monolithic category, while in fact, it is important to point out that the Manhattan stores that she has visited only cater to a very small, affluent elite. Only select stores house the brands she has enumerated. And only even more select stores, the likes of Bergdorf Goodman or Chanel, would have a salesperson wearing a Chanel dress.[66] A brief visit to Target or WalMart would reveal sprawling "plus-size" sections for women and men. In other words, Mernissi is basing her conclusions about Western women on a very limited group that does not represent the heterogeneity of American women, much less Western women, not to mention that such stores have an important clientele from outside the West, wealthy Middle Easterners included, which will be addressed in chapter 4.

Although she temporarily shifts the discussion to Western women, Mernissi's main focus is still Muslim women. By establishing that Western women are confined to a harem that celebrates youthful looks and small sizes, Mernissi seeks to show that Muslim women are better off than women in the West: "These Western attitudes, I thought, are even more dangerous and cunning than the Muslim ones because the weapon used against women is time. [. . .] This Western time-defined veil is even crazier than the space-defined one enforced by the Ayatollahs."[67] It is important to note that Mernissi is not alone in comparing Muslim and Western ways of confining and masking women's bodies. The Egyptian feminist Nawal El Saadawi, who has condemned the veil on many occasions, is very critical of women who wear makeup. She writes that she never hid her face "under make-up or powder, or pastes of any kind" because she "did not believe in a femininity born with slave society and handed down to us with class and patriarchy."[68]

Comparison of patriarchies can be productive in the sense that such exercise could potentially invite alliances between women and feminists of different religions and cultures. The comparisons above, however, are not productive when they are used as an apology for patriarchal oppression. In her narrative, Mernissi invents a Muslim culture in which women's bodies are embraced regardless of shape or size. She informs the salesperson that she doesn't even know her size:

> I come from a country where there is no size for women's clothes. [. . .] I buy my own material and the neighborhood seamstress or craftsman makes me the silk or leather skirt I want. They just take my measurements each time I see them. Neither the seamstress nor I know exactly

what size my new skirt is. [. . .] No one cares about my size in Morocco as long as I pay taxes on time.

The saleswoman responds that Mernissi should advertize her "country as a paradise for stressed working women."[69] It is difficult to know if one should take Mernissi's statements as fact or fiction. Her conclusion, however, does not leave any room for ambiguity: "I realized for the first time that maybe 'size 6' is a more violent restriction imposed on women than is the Muslim veil." By the end of the encounter, as she delights in telling the tale, which verges on narcissism, of a superior land uncorrupted by Western ideals, Mernissi affirms her superiority over the Western woman. Mernissi may have sought to challenge Western myths about Muslim women, but she ends up instituting a new one according to which Muslim women are heterosexual, confident, free from the restrictions of size, diet, and other beauty myths, and ultimately superior to women in the West.

MERNISSI AND U.S. FOREIGN POLICY

Though popular and populist, Islamic feminism is ultimately unproductive. Reinterpreting texts, celebrating resistance, and criticizing the West have not been conducive to gender equality in the predominantly Muslim societies. While Mernissi may have realized in the high-end Manhattan store "how the image of beauty in the West can hurt and humiliate a woman as much as the veil does when enforced by the state police in extremist nations such as Iran, Afghanistan, or Saudi Arabia",[70] the truth still remains that not all women in the West wear make-up, and far fewer can don a size 6, whether they desire it or not. Many women and girls in Iran, Afghanistan, and Saudi Arabia, on the other hand, are veiled, regardless of what they would prefer. Even today, Muslim women are jailed, stoned, and lashed for not complying with traditional Islamic dress. Women in Pakistan are attacked with acid for not fulfilling their husbands' wishes. Women in Algeria have endured the wrath of Islamism for years during the country's civil war and beyond. Women in Afghanistan have been mutilated, deprived of education, raped, and imprisoned in the name of religion and tradition. Ironically, the authors of these atrocities, just like Mernissi and many other Islamic feminists, also call for a return to an authentic religion before its corruption by the West, by colonialism, imperialism, and other forces that supposedly seek to undermine Islam and Muslims.

Even in Muslim countries often considered "less conservative," Islamic feminism has not succeeded in changing laws that affect women's justice and dignity. In spite of Mernissi's work and that of other feminists, there are still laws which give the man who rapes a minor the option of *marrying* her in order to avoid a prison term of one to five years.

Any rapist in his right mind would take the deal, and they do, leaving girls to endure domestic abuse in the legitimate institution of marriage, where marital rape is not viewed as a crime. Following the highly publicized case of Amina Filali's suicide after she was forced to marry her rapist, there were discussions about possible amendments to the rape-marriage law, which is certainly a step in the right direction. It is also a positive example of what can be accomplished when those in the West lend support to feminists within Muslim countries who fight to improve women's lives. However, even if this particular law were to change, there are many more laws that discriminate against women simply because they are women. Article 39 of the *Moudawwana*, or Moroccan family code, does not recognize marriage between a Muslim woman and a non-Muslim man. Article 453 of the penal code prohibits abortion. As unjust as they are, these laws find their justification in the same religious texts and traditions that Islamic feminists so desperately try to reinterpret. For after all, the legal system in Morocco, as in most other predominantly Muslim countries, is strongly influenced by *sharia*. However, as dire as the situation of women in Morocco may appear based on the examples cited here, it bears repeating that Morocco, relatively speaking, is one of the least conservative Muslim nations.

Yet it is understandable why in a post-9/11 world Mernissi's work, along with that of Islamic feminists, may be seductive. It reassures those who fear "Western domination," both Muslims and non-Muslims, that Muslims are self-sufficient, that they do not need Western ideologies and values, and that organic change can come from within. There are scholars who see Islamic feminism as an ally in a democratic and anti-imperialist agenda.[71] Moreover, it is reassuring to some that Muslim women will seek justice but will continue to be Muslim women, respectful of culture, tradition, and the sacred texts. They will continue to veil, to respect their elders, to protect their virginity, to serve their husbands, and to dedicate themselves to their children and homes. In sum, Islamic feminism is harmless because it is not a transformative feminism, but rather an explicative feminism: it explains why Islamic patriarchy is misunderstood; all that is needed is reinterpretation.

Western feminists, too, for the most part, as discussed in the next chapter, have been seduced by Islamic feminism. Part of the enthusiasm for Islamic feminism is more of a reaction of third wave feminists to accusations made of Western feminists from previous generations who have dared to interrogate patriarchy outside Western boundaries. Third wave feminists, influenced by postcolonial theory, have rejected what was described as the "gender universalism" of earlier so-called ethnocentric "white feminists,"[72] in favor of a more relativist and "inclusive" feminism.[73] Repeating Islamic feminist apologies is becoming the politically correct thing to do. The Western feminist's duty has therefore been reduced to "understanding" how what may appear as signs of oppression are *in their cultural contexts* symbols of emancipation.

This discourse has also infiltrated U.S. foreign policy and how foreign affairs policy makers view their responsibility vis-à-vis women outside the West. For example, Isobel Coleman, Director of the Council on Foreign Relations' Women and Foreign Policy program, is one of the most enthusiastic advocates of Islamic feminism, whose "Godmother" she insists, is Fatima Mernissi. Coleman writes:[74]

> The great potential of Islamic feminism is its grassroots appeal. Secular feminism—both in the Middle East and in the West—has always been the province of urban elites and intellectuals, and that has long been its greatest weakness. Social change takes time to make its way from city salons and urban newspapers to the countryside, especially in places with few roads and little public education. Because it strives to work within the values of Islam, not against them, Islamic feminism has the potential to be embraced by local leaders, perhaps most importantly by religious leaders [. . .] who can lend their authority to the difficult changes at hand.[75]

Coleman's position is understandable. From a strategic standpoint, it is easier to dialogue with religious leaders and secure a few rights for girls and women as long as one has no intention of "westernizing" these women. The idea is that for women in certain areas of the Muslim world, a few rights are better than none and it is more productive to make concessions to the Islamists in those areas for the sake of improving, even if minimally, the quality of life for these girls and women. It is true that minimizing suffering for women is indeed a noble goal. However, such approach imposes limits from the beginning on what a feminist movement should accomplish for Muslim women. It is problematic when women living in the West, enjoying the fruit of a long established feminist tradition, envision a limited potential for Muslim women. Many feminists in the West, though admittedly with an imperfect history in this regard, are still striving for an intersectional analysis of their cause that takes into account religion, sexual orientation, sexual practices, race, class, and marital status. And yet, Muslim women are repeatedly asked to settle for a world in which the best they can hope for is a compromised alliance with religious patriarchy. Are Muslim women not deserving of justice, dignity, the right to dress the way they wish, the right to marry whom they wish, and the right to have fulfilling sexual lives? When the priority of foreign affairs policy makers, too, shifts to searching for the silver lining in Muslim women's oppression, who then will protect the countless women in various parts of the Muslim world who are being stoned, whipped, harassed, raped, and denied education and opportunity simply for being born women?

Unfortunately, the apologetic narratives championed by some Western and Islamic feminists are not doing women or Muslim societies a service by holding them to lower standards. The West owes many of its accomplishments to a long history of unapologetic critique, including self-critique. Rather than encourage critique, Islamic feminists find it their job to defend and apologize. It is especially disheartening when, even scholars who were once intolerant of patriarchal oppression engage in what Lebanese feminist Mai Ghoussoub describes as "accommodation of obscurantism", as she writes:

> How many times, over successive generations, as the tides of religious fundamentalism (or opportunism) ebbed and flowed, have we seen women who were once courageous in their rejection of mystification and oppression eventually bow before them and on occasion even end by defending them! Fear of being accused of the contagion of "occidental values" all too easily leads to discovery of the superiority of the Harem, compared to Western marriage and adultery, as many examples show. Some of the most outstanding contemporary feminists, daunted by the scale of the task before them and the isolation in which they stand, have changed their tone recently.[76]

Feminists such as Fatima Mernissi, Nawal Saadawi and Leila Ahmed, who were once openly and unapologetically self-critical, are now celebrating patriarchal institutions as a source of empowerment for women. Chapter 4 continues this discussion about Islam and both Western and Islamic feminist critique, focusing on another myth: the veil as a liberating experience for women. To what extent can the veil in the Muslim world be considered a symbol of women's agency and empowerment?

NOTES

1. Miriam Cooke, *Women Claim Islam: Creating Islamic Feminism Through Literature* (New York: Routledge, 2001), 56.

2. Fatima Mernissi, *The Veil and the Male Elite: A Feminist Interpretation of Women's Rights in Islam*, trans. Mary Jo Lakeland (Reading: Addison-Wesley, 1991), 115.

3. Ibid., 81.

4. As Jamila Bargach puts it, "Composed from the perspective of Islamic 'light' (*'asr an-nur*), pre-Islamic practices and traditions were described to result from the sway of 'ignorant' spirit, the pre-Islamic period itself being labeled *'asr al-jahiliyya*, era of ignorance." Bargach, *Orphans of Islam: Family, Abandonment, and Secret Adoption in Morocco* (New York: Rowman & Littlefield, 2002), 47.

5. Mernissi, *The Veil and the Male Elite*, 123–24.

6. Syafiq Hasiym, *Understanding Women in Islam: An Indonesian Perspective* (Jakarta: Solstice, 2006), 138.

7. Mernissi relies on the religious authority of Imam Malik to interrogate the authenticity of al-Bukhari's collection of "authentic" *hadith*: "What conclusion must one draw from this? That even the authentic Hadith must be vigilantly examined with a magnifying glass? That is our right, Malik Ibn Anas tells us. Al-Bukhari, like all the fuqaha, began his work of collecting by asking for Allah's help and acknowledging that only He is infallible." Mernissi, *The Veil and Male Elite*, 76.

8. Ibid., 72.
9. Ibid., 80–81.
10. Ibid., 72.
11. Ibid., 86–87.
12. Mernissi explains that "[f]or some theologians the *hijab* is punishment. This is the case with al-Nisaburi: Among the invocations recited by al-Siriy al-Siqti, we can point out the following: 'God if Thou must torture me with something, don't torture me with the humiliation of the *hijab*.' " Ibid., 97.
13. Ibid., 97.
14. "And say to the believing women that they should lower their gaze and guard their modesty; that they should not display their beauty and ornaments except what (must ordinarily) appear thereof; that they should draw their veils over their bosoms and not display their beauty except to their husbands, their fathers, their husband's fathers, their sons, their husband's sons, their brothers or their brothers' sons, er their sisters' sons, or their women, or the slaves whom their right hands possess, or male servants free of physical needs, or small children who have no sense of the shame of sex; and that they should not strike their feet in order to draw attention to their hidden ornaments." Qur'an, 24:31.
15. Hammed Shahidian, *Women in Iran: Emerging Voices in the Women's Movement* (Westport: Greenwood Press, 2002), 74.
16. Mernissi, *The Veil and the Male Elite*, 105.
17. Ibid., 118.
18. See Hatoon Ajwad al-Fassi, *Women in Pre-Islamic Arabia: Nabataea* (Oxford: British Archaeological Reports International Series, 2007).
19. Leila Ahmed, *Women and Gender in Islam: Historical Roots of a Modern Debate* (New Haven: Yale University Press, 1992), 42.
20. Ibid., 43.
21. Mernissi, *The Veil and the Male Elite*, 117–18.
22. For example in her earlier work, Mernissi was more ambivalent vis-à-vis Muhammad's marriage with Zaynab, his adoptive son's wife. She wrote that the Prophet's passion for his daughter-in-law was "scandalous, by his own people's standards" especially since "In Muhammad's Arabia, the link created by adoption was considered identical to blood-ties." Mernissi, *Beyond the Veil: Male-Female Dynamics in Modern Muslim Society* (1975; Bloomington: Indiana University Press, 1987), 56.
23. Amina Wadud, *Qur'an and Woman: Rereading the Sacred Text from a Woman's Perspective* (New York: Oxford University Press, 1999), 74.
24. Ibid., 76.
25. Jamila Hussain, *Islam, Its Law and Society* (Sydney: Federation Press, 2003), 144–55.
26. Fatima Mernissi, *Dreams of Trespass: Tales of Harem Girlhood* (Reading: Addison-Wesley, 1994), 151.
27. Ibid., 109.
28. Ibid., 59.
29. Ibid., 207.
30. Mernissi, *Dreams of Trespass*, 143.
31. Ibid., 127.
32. Mernissi, *Dreams of Trespass*, 194.
33. Ibid., 33.
34. Ibid., 9.
35. Nawal El Saadawi, A Daughter of Isis: The Autobiography of Nawal El Saadawi, trans. Sherif Hetata (London: Zed Books, 1999), 7.
36. Leila Ahmed, *A Border Passage: From Cairo to America—A Woman's Journey* (New York: Farrar, Straus and Giroux, 1999), 123.
37. Ibid., 125.
38. Mernissi, *The Veil and the Male Elite*, 62.
39. Mernissi, *Dreams of Trespass*, 3.

40. Ibid., 226.

41. Ibid., 154.

42. Ibid., 113.

43. Ibid., 17.

44. Hasna Lebbady, "Fatima Mernissi's *Dreams of Trespass*: Self Representation or Confinement within the Discourse of Otherness," in *North-South Linkages and Connections in Continental and Diaspora African Literatures*, ed. Edris Makward, Mark Lilleleht, and Ahmed Saber (Trenton: Africa World Press, 2005), 133.

45. Lebbady situates Mernissi's narrative in the context of the Orientalist discourse criticized by Said: "The discourse Mernissi uses conforms with the notion of the Orient which Edward Said reveals in his *Orientalism* to be a construct of the European mind. Similarly, it appears to conform with the patriarchal view of woman as Other which has been contested by feminist discourse ever since Simone de Beauvoir's seminal thesis that one is not born a woman but becomes one. In fact, although Mernissi attempts to present a specifically feminist perspective of Morocco, she does not appear to critique either imperialist or patriarchal discourse, but rather to accept their norms without question, making her position appear to be rather ambiguous." Ibid., 130.

46. Fatima Mernissi, *Scheherazade Goes West: Different Cultures, Different Harems* (New York: Washington Square Press, 2001), 109.

47. Ibid., 2.

48. Ibid., 13.

49. Ibid., 12.

50. Ibid., 14.

51. Ibid., 14–15.

52. Ibid., 23.

53. It is interesting to note that in her work Mernissi privileges examples of Medieval Islamic literature from the East at the expense of examples from al-Andalus such as the thirteenth-century tale *Hadith Bayad wa Riyad* discussed in the first chapter.

54. Mernissi, *Scheherazade Goes West*, 125.

55. Ibid., 171.

56. Ibid., 99–101.

57. Al-Nafzaoui, *The Perfumed Garden of the Cheikh Nefzaoui: A Manual of Arabian Erotology*, 100–101.

58. See Ahmad al-Tifashi, *The Delight of Hearts, or What You Will Not Find in Any Book*. Trans. Edward A. Lacey (San Francisco: Gay Sunshine Press, 1988), 109–10.

59. Ibid., 179–180.

60. *Hammam al-Malatily*, dir. Salah Abouseif (Ehab Elleissi Films Cairo, 1973).

61. Mernissi, *Scheherazade Goes West*, 102.

62. Ibid., 101.

63. Ibid., 211–12.

64. Frank Gargione, "Plus-Sized Fashion at Saks: Some Background," *Racked* 29 July 2010, available at http://ny.racked.com/archives/2010/07/29/plussized_fashion_at_saks_some_insight.php (25 November 2012).

65. For an elaborate discussion of class in Mernissi's work in general, see Raja Rhouni, *Secular and Islamist Feminist Critiques in the Work of Fatima Mernissi* (Leiden: Brill, 2010), 77–118.

66. Mernissi describes the saleswoman as wearing a "knee-length, navy blue, Chanel dress." *Scheherazade Goes West*, 212.

67. Ibid., 214.

68. El Saadawi, A Daughter of Isis, 7.

69. Mernissi, *Scheherazade Goes West*, 212–13.

70. Mernissi, *Scheherazade Goes West*, 208.

71. See Anouar Majid, "The Politics of Islamic Feminism," *Signs: Journal of Women and Culture in Society* 23.1(1998): 321–61.

72. Benitha Roth, *Separate Roads to Feminism: Black, Chicana, and White Feminist Movements in America's Second Wave* (New York: Cambridge University Press, 2004), 188.

73. See Michele Barrett and Anne Phillips, "Introduction," *Destabilizing Theory: Contemporary Feminist Debates*, ed. Barrett and Phillips (Cambridge: Polity Press, 1992).

74. Isobel Coleman, *Paradise Beneath Her Feet: How Women Are Transforming the Middle East* (New York: Random House, 2010), 36.

75. Ibid., xix.

76. See Mai Ghoussoub, "Feminist—or the Eternal Masculine—in the Arab World," *New Left Review* 161 (1987): 3–18.

FOUR

Veiled Apologies

Muslim Women and the Truth about Choice

When it comes to the veil, feminist scholarship has largely focused on two particular arguments. One is the hermeneutic argument, namely the study of religious texts including the Qur'an, to decipher Islam's true position vis-à-vis the veil, as seen in the work of Mernissi. The other is the question of choice, namely whether women choose to veil or not. Examining religious texts is quite an endeavor; establishing that it is a woman's choice to veil is not as demanding. With the rare exceptions of countries such as Iran and Saudi Arabia where women must cover, it is assumed that most Muslim women in the rest of the world veil out of "choice." A woman's personal decision to cover her head or face is accepted without question, even by feminists who have made a career out of questioning assumed choices.

This chapter does not address the theological explanation of the veil and whether it is a religious obligation or not as it would be beyond its scope. Nor does it deny that women often wear the veil without direct and explicit pressure from their immediate male relatives. Instead, I turn to a discussion of the supposed liberating function of the veil. What was once critiqued by feminists, Muslim and non-Muslim alike, as a symbol of oppression became, particularly in the post-9/11 era, praised as a means for women's emancipation within Islam and resistance to the West and its values. It has been argued that "because of capitalism's emphasis on the body and on materiality, wearing the *hijab* can be an empowering and liberating experience for women."[1] It is often repeated that the veil allows for women to be "recognized as individuals who are admired for their mind and personality, 'not for their beauty or lack of it.'"[2] The veil, in the words of a non-Muslim writer "is not about shame of the female body, as Western feminists sometimes insist, but about claiming their bodies."[3] This chapter interrogates these claims. The first section argues that the veil has not made Muslim women immune to consumerism nor has it protected them from the fashion industry. The second and third sections consider the concept of "choice." Through discussion of the first film dedicated primarily to the veil, *Hijab al-hob* (Veil of Love) (2008) by Aziz Salmy, I argue that while women in Morocco are usually not forced to wear the veil, societal pressures as well as the patriarchy's anxious relations with the feminine body coerce women into veiling.

NAOMI WOLF AND THE APOLOGY FOR THE VEIL

It is often argued that Western feminists do not understand Islam, which they are quick to dismiss as an oppressive, patriarchal religion. It has also been claimed that Western feminist discourse has paved the way for military invasions by portraying Muslim women as oppressed, veiled women in need of "saving."[4] And yet Western feminists who defend Islamic institutions such as the veil have not received an equal share of criticism, though their message is just as problematic, simplistic, and even contradictory to their feminist engagement. This is the case with Naomi Wolf. Regarded as a spokesperson for third wave feminism, Wolf established herself by criticizing the fashion and cosmetics industries for creating unattainable beauty standards that lead to a conflictive relationship between a woman and her body. In her popular book, *The Beauty Myth: How Images of Beauty Are Used Against Women*, Wolf writes that women must have the uncoerced choice to do whatever they want with their bodies and their appearance without being judged or punished. Wolf insists on a woman's right to choose when it comes to her body and sexuality, as when she writes:

> A woman wins by giving herself and other women permission—to eat; to be sexual; to age; to wear overalls, a paste tiara, a Balenciaga gown, a second-hand opera cloak, or combat boots; to cover up or to go practically naked; to do whatever we choose in following—or ignoring—our own aesthetic. A woman wins when she feels that what each woman does with her own body—unforced, uncoerced—is her own business.[5]

When the subject of critique is Western women, therefore, Wolf is not ready to make any concessions in the name of religion, culture, or tradition.

In the post-9/11 era, Wolf's feminist discourse has shifted radically, at least as far as Muslim women are concerned. Rather than analyzing how the beauty myth affects Muslim women, Wolf veils them behind myths of empowerment and liberation. She imagines that Muslim women living outside the West are immune to Western obsessions and vices: confident with their bodies and sexuality not in spite of, but rather thanks to, their liberating veils. In "Behind the Veil Lives a Thriving Muslim Sexuality," published in *The Sydney Morning Herald* on August 30, 2008, Wolf adds yet another article to the plethora of writing about what Muslim women *truly* wear beneath their veils.[6] She asks: "But are we in the West radically misinterpreting Muslim sexual mores, particularly the meaning to many Muslim women of being veiled or wearing the chador? And are we blind to our own markers of the oppression and control of women?" Wolf goes on to narrate her own tale of travels to Morocco, Jordan, and Egypt revealing to the West the truth about Muslim women's veils and sexuality. As she is invited "to join a discussion in women-only settings within Muslim homes," Wolf learns that "Muslim attitudes toward women's appearance and sexuality are not rooted in repression, but in a strong sense of public versus private, of what is due to God and what is due to one's husband." Inside the home "in the context of marital intimacy, Victoria's Secret, elegant fashion and skin care lotions abounded." Wolf is shown wedding videos "with sensuous dancing that the bride learns as part of what makes her a wonderful wife, and which she proudly displays for her bridegroom, suggesting that sensuality was not alien to Muslim women." In the public sphere, however, Moroccan, Jordanian, and Egyptian women prefer to wear a "chador or the headscarf," which they do not view as a form of subjugation. Rather, they feel "liberated from what they experienced as the intrusive, commodifying, basely sexualizing Western gaze." In fact, many women confessed to her that when they wear "Western clothes," they feel objectified, "on display," and forced to measure themselves "against the standards of models in magazines, which are hard to live up to." On the other hand, when they wear the scarf, they "feel respected" and people relate to them "as an individual, not an object." To better understand these women, Wolf wears a "shalwar kameez and a headscarf" and heads to a Moroccan "bazaar." To her surprise, she felt free: "as I moved about the market—the curve of my breasts covered, the shape of my legs obscured, my long hair not flying about me—I felt a novel sense of calm and serenity. I felt, yes, in certain way, free." Wolf concludes her article with the benefits of women's veiling and private sexuality. She argues that Muslim and Orthodox Jewish women have more intense and fulfilling sexual lives with their husbands than "is common in the West." The rationale is that the husband does not see women, including his wife, "half-naked all day long." Wolf concedes that she does not mean "to dismiss the many women leaders in the Muslim world who regard veiling as a means of controlling women." But "choice," she insists, "is everything." The moral of the story is that women in a Western culture in which "women are not so free to age, to be respected as mothers, workers or spiritual beings, and to disregard Madison Avenue" should not consider themselves any less repressed than a veiled Muslim woman.[7]

Although a notion of choice may exist in some contexts, this is not justification for the refusal to apply a feminist critique toward the veil. As Marnia Lazreg points out, "The hidden premise of the apologetic approach is that the veil is unquestionable because its wearers purportedly assume it to be so, and as long as they 'choose' it, our task as researchers is to reveal its benefits for *them*." Lazreg also highlights a more recent trend in the discourse about the veil, by which the veil "emerges as a field of struggle, not only between men and women, as it has been historically, but also between native women (opposed to it) and women from non-Muslim cultures, or those hailing from Muslim cultures who support veiling in one way or another."[8] Wolf contributes to this trend of singing the virtues of veiling at a time when scholars such as Lazreg call for a more complex analysis.

Unfortunately, Wolf is not alone. Others have conflated the defense of the veil and the fight against Islamophobia. Australian writer and radio personality Helen Razer writes that "at least women in burqas are not judged on their looks."[9] Madeleine Bunting argues that Muslim women "do not wish to express their sexuality in public" by wearing revealing clothes; instead they "believe that its proper place is in the privacy of a relationship."[10] Germaine Greer, who criticized the bikini as a "disfiguring garment," joked that "Nobody's bum ever looked big in a burqa," and that since ninety percent of women look "dreadful in a bikini", they should either "stay home or wear some version of the burqa on a beach."[11] While they attempt to explore the heterogeneous nature of the Muslim woman's experience, Wolf, Razer, Bunting, and Greer seem to forget that women in the West have more clothing options than a bikini. Moreover, while these scholars imagine Muslim societies as belonging to another space and time, before corruption by Western obsession with beauty, thinness, and fashion, the reality is that Muslim women from Morocco to Iran are not immune to the quest for beauty, even when it is destructive.[12] Multi-million dollar industries in Muslim countries are dedicated to helping women attain "the perfect body." Wolf's stay in Morocco may not have been long, but how could she have missed the large billboard advertisements for gyms all over the boulevards of Moroccan cities? In recent years there has been an increase in sports centers which vary from the small, working-class neighborhood gyms to city-like sport centers with cafes and restaurants, such as the Sport Plazza in Casablanca, whose two branches cover seven acres of the city, making it, as its website brags, the biggest sports club in Africa and the second biggest in the world.[13] Far from an exclusive concern with health, the advertisements for these gyms, which are easily accessible through their websites and Facebook pages, sell an ideal of feminine beauty not different from the Western ideal.[14] In Muslim countries, as in the West, we encounter those who prefer quicker results, electing plastic surgery instead. A Google search for "chirurgie esthétique au Maroc" will bring up countless plastic surgery clinics, mostly in Casablanca and Rabat. While many of them cater to a foreign clientele, Muslims and non-Muslims alike, looking for package deals that combine surgery and the beach, Moroccans, both women and men from different economic classes, form the majority of patients in these clinics.[15]

Similarly, the West is not the sole victim of the fashion industry. It should not come as a surprise to anyone that whether they are wearing the veil or not, women with an interest in fashion around the world recognize the same iconic designers and brands. Anyone who walks down Paris' Avenue Montaigne and through the neighboring area in August, when Parisians have abandoned the city, will realize that it is populated mainly by veiled women, mostly though not exclusively from countries of the Gulf, who are keeping the Hermès, Chanel, Dior, Louis Vuitton, and Louboutin stores open. The self-proclaimed "world's largest themed shopping mall," named after the fourteenth-century Moroccan scholar and traveler Ibn Battuta (1304–1377), is in Dubai, catering to Muslim and non-Muslim women and men in search of high-end luxury goods.[16] The most recent addition to the world of luxury shopping is Morocco Mall in Casablanca, described as "the largest shopping mall in the Mediterranean basin and Africa."[17] Cities around the Arabo-Muslim world have established themselves as vibrant fashion capitals where trends are created and appropriated, as chronicled by street-style photographers such as Joseph Ouechen, whose website "You Are the Style" has become Morocco's leading fashion blog.[18] With the increase in the number of women veiling, multi-million dollar fashion businesses are now targeting this market. One of the most important textile companies in Morocco has opened 16 stores all over the country catering to their large clientele of veiled women.[19] It is therefore surprising to read that Wolf hadn't expected Moroccan women to wear Victoria's Secret underwear. Wolf did not even need to visit Muslim countries to become aware of the complex reality of the veil. A quick YouTube search will bring up the numerous channels dedicated to fashionable ways of wearing the veil.[20] Though Wolf and her followers may think otherwise, women in Morocco and elsewhere in Muslim countries are not freed from concerns of status, fashion, and the media simply because they veil.

Wolf's "surprise" at what she finds under Muslim women's veils betrays a narcissistic view of the West as having the sole claim to fashion. She simply assumes that the West is where fashion exists and that it belongs to Westerners. This arrogant perception also extends to imagining the West as the origin of vices:

> Among healthy young men in the West, who grow up on pornography and sexual imagery on every street corner, reduced libido is a growing epidemic, so it is easy to imagine the power that sexuality can carry in a more modest culture. And it is worth understanding the positive expe-

riences that women—and men—can have in cultures where sexuality is more conservatively directed.[21]

As chapter 1 indicates, long before there was a multi-billion dollar pornography industry in the San Fernando Valley of southern California, Muslims wrote and read texts that fulfilled, among others, a pornographic function for men. Interest in adult entertainment among Muslims persists today. According to Google Trends, which allows a user to type in a term and discover where in the world and with what frequency other people have searched for the same word, between January 2004 and August 2010, Muslim countries, including Muslim francophone countries such as Morocco and Algeria, were among the top countries in the world with the most queries for "sex" (English spelling) and "sexe" (French spelling).[22] Around the month of Ramadan every year, the trend shows a sharp drop in sex/sexe Google searches in Muslim-majority countries for which there is data available.[23] Moreover, in addition to being consumers of pornographic materials, Muslims are also producers. Although pornography is illegal in most Muslim countries, there are famous Muslim women and men working in the pornographic industry. One of the most recognized pornographic actresses in France is a Moroccan-born Muslim woman, Hafida El Khabchi, known by the stage name Yasmine Lafitte.

As these and many other examples show, the veil does not liberate Muslim societies from the "vice" of pornography, nor does it liberate Muslim women from capitalist consumerism, issues of self-esteem regarding the body, or even obsession with fashion. However, what is most disheartening about Wolf's perception of Muslim societies and Muslim women is not its inaccuracy. Wolf, certainly, is a staunch advocate for Western women's unconditional right to choose beyond the boundaries of patriarchy. Yet, when it comes to Muslim women, Wolf inadvertently enters into a coalition with patriarchy and defends its institutions, including the veil and heterosexual marriage, leading to many questions: If it is so important to contain sexuality in public spaces, as Wolf claims, why is it that Muslim men are not asked to veil? Is it because Wolf does not believe that Muslim women are capable of being sexually aroused by an unveiled man? What about women's physical and sexual attraction to other women? Does Wolf, along with those who defend the veil as a safeguard of intimacy, agree with Iranian president Mahmoud Ahmadinejad that homosexuality exists only in the West? What about sexuality in general; do Muslim women not have the right to claim their sexual agency, or are they condemned to sex within the "legitimate" boundaries of heterosexual marriage? Does the Muslim woman not desire anything other than these options? Does Wolf believe that women in the Muslim world deserve less than women in the West?

HIJAB AL-HOB, THE VEIL, AND PATRIARCHAL COERCION

Hijab al-hob (Veil of Love), which was described as a "Moroccan-style *Sex and the City*," is Aziz Salmy's first full-length feature. It is also the first Moroccan film that explicitly problematizes the veil, focusing more on its function in Moroccan society rather than its significance as a strictly religious symbol. It tells the story of five professional women living in Casablanca, brought together by friendship.[24] The protagonist, Batoul (Hayet Belhalloufi), is a beautiful twenty-eight-year old woman physician in love with Hamza (Younes Megri), who makes it clear that he has no desire to marry again, nor does he promise her a monogamous relationship. Hamza—who has lived for many years in Europe but is forced to return to Morocco due to his mother's illness—has already been married to a French woman, with whom he had a daughter. Until her encounter with Hamza, Batoul has been what in the Muslim patriarchal context would be described as an exemplary woman: an obedient daughter "protective" of her virginity. Her time outside her family and work is spent mostly in the company of her women friends. Meeting Hamza marks the beginning of an identity crisis as she finds herself torn between her "principles" and her sexual desires. To relieve her guilty conscience, she decides to put on the veil in public, while, in private, she continues to meet and have sex with her lover. The secrecy of her relationship eventually comes to an end when Batoul's brother spots the couple at a party. Batoul escapes in a car with Hamza but her brother chases them at high-speed, which leads to an accident that takes his life. Interpreting it as a divine punishment for her transgressions, Batoul stops seeing Hamza, and once again, she takes refuge in religion, praying and reading the Qur'an. The separation from her lover, however, does not last long. She returns to him and gets pregnant. Hamza refuses to marry her and she refuses to have an abortion. The protagonist's depressing story of *Hijab al-hob* provides a drastic contrast to the image of the veiled Muslim woman portrayed in the celebratory work of scholars such as Naomi Wolf.

Inside Morocco, *Hijab al-hob* was viewed as a direct attack on Islam, beginning with its title, which associates a religious symbol with profane love. In an interview published in a Moroccan newspaper a Moroccan imam and a member of Parliament, called for the boycott of the film because, in addition to tarnishing the image of veiled women, it could be a bad influence on young Muslim women.[25] The then general secretary of the Islamist party PJD (Justice and Development Party) who went on to become the country's Prime Minister in 2011, blamed "zionist influence," as zionism is often blamed whenever a filmmaker dares to show a kiss or addresses a topic judged taboo by Islamists.[26] Interestingly, neither the imam nor the general secretary had seen the film before they made these statements, which, as Salmy explains, is "revolting" particularly since they are supposed to represent Moroccans in parliament.[27] The film provoked anger even beyond Morocco. In an interview, Salmy mentioned that in some Arab countries, where the film was never officially screened, Islamists called for his punishment.[28] In spite of the controversy, the film performed well at the box office. It is also one of the most viewed Moroccan films available on YouTube.

Hijab al-hob destabilizes the apologetic discourse about the veil's empowering effect which has been advanced by many Islamists and Western feminists alike. Salmy argues that the veil is a mere fashion accessory that does not stand for anything:

> Wearing the veil has become very fashionable. Girls wear it as a fashion accessory: some use it to flirt with men, others for religious reasons. Nowadays, the Islamic shops flourish and offer a wide range of scarves. Needless to say, it is completely hypocritical to be offended that I use veiled actresses in my movie. This piece of cloth doesn't symbolize anything. There is nothing sacred about it. It is as if a girl who puts it on were to instantly become a saint. But the clothes do not make the monk and the scarf doesn't make you a good Muslim. I know many Moroccan women who cover themselves with scarves and at the same time hide a thousand and one flirtations. This is not a crime, it's just life.[29]

The veil does not liberate these Casablanca women. Rather, as Salmy insists, these upper-middle-class women drape themselves in the latest Dior and Bulgari to visually distinguish themselves by class and status.

However, though Salmy trivializes the veil, this does not mean that the reasons behind veiling are trivial. Although the women portrayed in the film are not *coerced* (none of his characters veil for primarily religious reasons, nor do they veil because their father, husband, or boyfriend force them to) it does not follow that their decision to don the *hijab* should necessarily be celebrated as a manifestation of choice and agency. One of the characters, for example, is open about her reason: she puts on the veil in order to find a husband. As she explains, "Women who put on the veil get married faster." Another one confirms: "So what! What is wrong with that? I admit it. I wear the veil in order to find a husband and also because I am [religiously] convinced." But Nawal, Batoul's friend and colleague, is clear about her reasons and does not attempt to pass them off as religious: "Me, I don't have any real conviction. I just want to start a family but I am afraid that no husband will come and I will become everyone's laughing stock." When Houyam, the rebelling mother who prefers colorful wigs to scarves, insists that if she were forced into wearing the veil she would shave her head before being made to look like a "crow," Nawal responds: "crow or ninja, I can't wait to have pictures of my kids on my desk [at work]."[30] As the film develops, it reveals the length to which Nawal is ready to go in order to get married. She is willing to settle for a religiously conservative man, such as Anas, who does not listen to music because he believes it to be against his religion, and greets women by shaking their hands without looking them in the eyes.

Why would a lively, smart, and accomplished woman such as Nawal settle for a depressing man who does not listen to music? It has to do with society's double standards, as she explains, in which men who age are considered more mature, while women are viewed as "old maids." Nawal also has a physical disability that she fears makes her less desirable as a wife than the more attractive Batoul. The religious man for a woman such as Nawal is therefore a fallback option, when everything else fails. She jokes that if she does not succeed in meeting the "Moroccan Richard Gere", she will marry a "bearded" man. Religious men, it seems from the attitude of the women in the film, are easy to manipulate. Blinded by the mentality of the permissible versus the forbidden, *halal* versus *haram*, the religious man is viewed as easier to trick because of his inability to doubt or be skeptical. For example, when Batoul puts on the veil during Ramadan, Anas automatically assumes it is a sign of repentance and return to the "right" path. A veil not only hides a woman's hair from the public, but also serves to mask her true self from men, including her husband.

However, to understand the concessions that highly educated and financially independent women are ready to make, and the ruses to which they resort in order to marry, it is important to look at the significance of marriage in the context of Moroccan society. In Morocco, regardless of their social status, unmarried women are confronted with many obstacles that limit their access to power. As Fatima Sadiqi explains, Moroccan women's social status and identity depend to a great extent on their marital status. Legally speaking, women are not considered "free agents" since they depend on their fathers and husbands. The value put on marriage, as Sadiqi points out, affects the experiences of women as citizens within Morocco:

> The social value attributed to married women is due to the fact that marriage is strongly encouraged by Islam, a particularly powerful component Moroccan culture. Marriage and family are sacred as they constitute very powerful means of social control and a guarantee for stability and continuity. Marriage is not only encouraged by religion, but it is reinforced and consolidated by institutions. From a very early age and through their schooling, girls are constantly reminded that their ultimate aim in life is to secure a husband and raise a family. Being educated and having a job are "secondary" aims that "complete" and never replace marriage. As a result, society views married women (wives and mothers) positively and considers them more "successful" and more "trustworthy" than unmarried women. In turn, married women derive social identity and social power from this status. They generally feel more socially secure than unmarried women. In fact, many girls shun

from furthering their higher studies, especially outside Morocco, lest their chances of being married slip away from them. This is reinforced by the fact that men, in general, are reluctant to marry girls and women who have completed their higher studies outside Morocco as these are generally believed to be "too independent," "experienced," "harder to deal with," and far from being obedient.[31]

The "experience" to which Sadiqi is referring is not merely professional experience, but also extends to sexual experience. Regardless of a woman's accomplishment, anxiety over the "loss" of a woman's virginity before marriage continues to haunt Moroccan women and men of all socioeconomic categories. Education and professional accomplishments thus become a double-edged sword for women. On the one hand, they allow them to become less dependent on a man financially, and on the other, independence marginalize women as they are no longer desired as wives. This is the dilemma that women in *Hijab al-hob* face. Their professional, economical, and intellectual accomplishments are trivialized because they are not married. When Nawal comments that she and the women her age are competing with sixteen-year-old girls for men, Houyam responds that teenagers find husbands because they do not waste their time studying. In such an environment that devalues women who are not married, it is therefore not surprising that as a final resort, these women decide to put on the veil in order to find a husband.

The situation described in *Hijab al-hob* is not unusual but rather common throughout Morocco, particularly in urban centers. As Salmy explains, the film is inspired by the reality of "independent women, who have a house, a job, a car, who are emancipated, frequent the men they want," but who, "past a certain age, decide to wear the veil, thinking it will help them find a husband."[32] But how could the veil, when worn in such circumstances, be said to liberate women? How could feminists sing the praises of the veil when women are coerced into veiling by a patriarchal society that has an uneasy relationship with educated, empowered, and independent women? The veil in this context undermines everything that the feminist movement has attempted to achieve. It is a way of apologizing to those who fear women's accomplishments, for it communicates that, in spite of their cars and houses, professions and bank accounts, college degrees and intellect, they are still women. The veil becomes a concession through which women reaffirm their subordination in a society where they cannot achieve equality.

THE VEIL AS A MEDIATED ACCESS TO PUBLIC SPACE

Clearly not all women who wear the veil do so in order to get married. Many married and unmarried women cover up in order to have easier access to public spaces. The veil in most Muslim societies functions as what anthropologist Hanna Papneck has termed "portable seclusion" or what Lila Abu-Lughod has described as "mobile homes."[33] The argument is that, far from denying women agency, the veil and its derivatives (the niqab, burqa, burkini, and others) allow women to move freely in societies that are suspicious of women's activities outside the domestic sphere. Katherine Bullock recounts how the veil facilitates women's movement in public spaces:

> Some of the women whom I interviewed [. . .] mentioned that a feature of *hijab* which they enjoyed was the increased respect and good treatment they received from men, even non-Muslim men. Women in other countries also mentioned this aspect of wearing *hijab* as a positive feature that they enjoyed. They find that the *hijab* succeeds in having men keep their distance because it creates a space cushion around a woman, even for a non-Muslim man who has no understanding of the reasoning behind *hijab*. In the Muslim context "wearing a veil represents purity of intention and behavior. It is a symbol affirming that 'I'm clean' and 'I'm not available.'" The effect of this personal space barrier gives women more freedom to travel through the public realm in peace, and in those Muslim countries that have an ideology of honor, husbands' jealousy, and parents' concerns are vitiated by *hijab*, giving the women more freedom to move around.

Bullock does not question the self-righteous statement about cleanliness nor does she interrogate the problematic use of such hygienic discourse in the context of the veil. If the veil sends the message that one is "clean" and "not available", is not wearing the veil an indication that one is "dirty" and "available"? Do "unclean" women who do not wear the veil and are harassed on the street or abused by a jealous husband "bring it on themselves"? Rather than address the serious implications of her statements and those of the women she interviews, Bullock goes on to claim that wearing the veil demonstrates that women "can participate in public life, while maintaining the Islamic dress code." She insists that the veil "can give a woman a sense of power and hence self-esteem." Oblivious to the fact that women in Iran must wear the veil, Bullock's apology extends to Iranian women as well, many of whom, she insists are "pleased with wearing *hijab*" because it helps them advance professionally.[34]

The apology that the veil supposedly makes it easier for women to occupy public space is problematic for many reasons. First, if women have to pay a price, namely veil, in order to participate in public spaces, then it is assumed that they are inferior to men, since it is a given that men can occupy public spaces without fearing aggression. Secondly, instead of holding street harassers accountable, the shame in such a confrontation is shifted to women based on what they do or do not wear. This is like blaming the rape victim for wearing revealing clothes. Moreover, it is easy to put such theory to the test. If Bullock's and others' claims were true, then women in countries where the veil is mandatory, such as Iran and Saudi Arabia, should be safe from harassment. The reality, however, is that women is these places, just as in the rest of the Muslim world, are not immune to aggression and violence in public spaces. Overwhelming evidence and accounts from these countries prove that the veil fails to protect women from harassment and sexual violence.[35]

These apologies for the veil find justification in women's productive occupation of public spaces (eg. work or study) but neglect to acknowledge the other reasons why women may be outside their homes. In other words, stepping outside the house seems to be always connected with a legitimate purpose. It has a beginning and an end, and is often framed within a specific bracket of time. Furthermore, most of these activities benefit others (husband, father, children) as much as they benefit the women themselves, if not more. Given the financial demands of maintaining a family, even the most extreme of extremists is not likely to object to having his wife contribute a paycheck to the household. Therefore, to celebrate the veil because it allows women to work outside the home fails to question whom women's work ultimately benefits. If money were not an issue, how many of these women, veiled or not, would be allowed to leave the house?

Attaching productivity and purpose to women's presence in public spaces also betrays the assumption that the domestic sphere remains the legitimate place of women, who, especially past a certain age, may step out on an exceptional basis and with an excuse or permission, to work, run errands, or go to school. However, they should not be on the street for the sole purpose of being on the street. The veil acts as a visual confirmation that aimless strolling, labeled *flânerie*, on the part of a woman, is problematic and depraved, that her leisurely presence in public spaces is illegitimate; in contrast to the domestic sphere where she can be herself and take off her "veils." Men, on the other hand, from an early age, are made to feel at home in the public arena whether with or without a purpose. In Morocco for example, there is the expression *rass derb*, literally "the head of the street," which refers to the entrance of one's street or neighborhood, where *wlad derb* or "the boys of the street or neighborhood" usually hang out;[36] regardless of their ages, boys occupy the street without need of justification. Over the years, *wlad derb* tend to form strong ties not only to each other but to the streets over which they are the guardians—this is especially true for lower-class and middle-class areas of a city or town because they have free access to the streets, whereas "clubs" and other spaces are reserved for the more affluent. In their neighborhoods' streets boys experiment with their male social identity. They become aware of the privileges granted to one merely for being born male. A boy or man can leave the house to be with friends and even stay out late without necessarily needing to ask for permission, whereas his sister needs to be *bent darhom*, literally the girl of *their* home, which designates a respectable woman who "elects" to be home rather than on the streets. The boys eventually become men and claim the rest of the city's streets. Anybody who travels through the Muslim world, whether in cities or rural areas, will encounter groups of men, of all ages and economic classes, spending time on the terraces of cafés, on street corners, or in the middle of the streets, playing soccer or other games, drinking coffee or tea, smoking cigarettes, consuming drugs, or engaging in an animated debate about the latest Barcelona vs. Real Madrid match. Meanwhile, the exemplary *bent darhom*, regardless of her economic class, skills, or education, is one who carries out her work in public spaces under various layers of "veils" and returns home, otherwise she may run the risk of being labeled *bent zenqa*, literally the girl of the street, or, in the Moroccan context, a prostitute. In short, as the linguistic expressions confirm, the male in the street is associated with protection and legitimacy, while the female is associated with a threat to order.

Unfortunately, when the veil becomes popular in a community, it exacerbates the conflictive relationship between women and the public arena, and even justifies violence against women. In recent years there have been numerous cases of aggression committed against women in Muslim societies for not wearing the veil. In Algeria in the 1990s, a large number of women and girls as young as fourteen were killed or forced into exile for having their heads exposed.[37] As recently as December 2011, in Algeria, two women were attacked with a tear gas bomb outside their university dorm for the same offense.[38] In the summer of 2012, the women of Tiznit, a small town in the south of Morocco, were terrorized by the attacks of *moul pekala*, or the one on the bicycle, a man who attacked women from behind with a knife. To make sure the injury resulted in a prominent scar, it is believed that he dipped the blade in garlic before committing his crimes. The targets of his attacks, which began a few days before Ramadan and continued throughout, were unveiled women and girls who wore jeans and skirts.[39] One can banalize this traumatizing crime by suggesting that it is an isolated incident not indicative of attitudes of the society at large. However, even when the attacks against unveiled women are committed by rogue criminals, these men act in an environment in which men have more legitimacy in public. This is not to say that women in societies where veiling is not the norm escape violence, nor does it mean that there was no violence against women before the rise in veiling. Where veiling becomes popular, however, a woman who doesn't is exposed to violence and harassment. One can legitimately ask if it can still be said that the women of Tiznit who decide to veil out of fear of *moul pekala* are doing so by *choice*. What does it mean to choose to wear the veil when one finds herself in situations in which she must either comply or be attacked? Would Wolf retain her celebratory discourse about the veil were she aware of its complexities?

Ironically, though not surprisingly, veiled women do not fare any better when it comes to enduring harassment and violence. As a "mobile home" the veil is a constant reminder that women's *natural* place is the home, and once it is established that being veiled is the *natural* state of women, it is difficult to delimit what constitutes enough veiling and when and how it should be reinforced. The most disheartening example is the tragic incident that resulted in the death of fifteen Saudi school girls, who were trapped inside their burning school. Witnesses reported seeing the Committee for the Promotion of Virtue and the Prevention of Vice, also known as the religious police or *Mutaween*, prevent the girls from leaving because they were not properly covered.[40] In Islamic countries with strict dress codes for women, women and girls are beaten for showing ankle in the street and at times even their "tempting" eyes in public.[41] In 2007, a cleric in al-Azhar University came to the conclusion that the veil did not provide enough separation between women and men. He issued a *fatwa* according to which women should breastfeed their adult male colleagues.[42] The rationale behind the *fatwa* is that according to Islamic tradition, even if a woman is not the biological mother, by breastfeeding a child she establishes a maternal relationship between the child and herself. By breastfeeding their adult colleagues, the cleric reasoned, the women would become their mothers, hence eliminating any possibility of a sexual relationship between women and their co-workers/sons. Such nonsensical logic is used as a justification for violating women and imposing more extreme limits on their bodies.

The problem with patriarchy, as with any tyrannical system, is that the more one complies, the more one is expected to comply. Even women who wear the veil and behave in a manner of which the religious and moral authorities approve, are not immune to suspicion. The authenticity of the veil and the motives behind veiling are constantly put to the test. A particularly telling example is "7ijab [hijab] Style" (veiled style), a song by Slam d'llah, a Rap group from Mohammedia, Morocco. The song describes a veiled woman who lies to her father making him believe that she is at the mosque, while in reality she is at a party drinking and enjoying the company of men:

> I'm a veiled girl, a little stylish
> Today I'm going to a party
> To dance a little
> I don't want to wear a jellaba
> I want jeans and high heels
> The hijab nowadays has become trendy
> The face covered with a quarter of a towel
> You look at her with her veil and you say that it is Islam
> You start talking to her about sex and she doesn't stop
> I tell you about one evening where there was this veiled woman
> She arrived in jellaba

Then she started taking her pleasure. [43]

This song summarizes well the inefficacy of the veil since even women who accede to the pressures of wearing it are regarded with suspicion and distrust.

This song reveals deep anxieties about women who deviate from the roles and spaces to which they are assigned. *Hijab al-hob* illustrates similar anxieties. The film may be compared to *Sex and the City*, but, while the latter's women characters are often seen strolling, four astride, dominating a welcoming New York City sidewalk, Casablanca's streets, on the other hand, are accurately depicted as far less hospitable to the casual woman window shopper. The five women friends of *Hijab al-hob* are never seen walking the city's streets. In one scene, they are shown jogging by the beach in the Corniche area of Casablanca. The Corniche, however, is to a great extent a marginal area occupied during the day by runners and beachgoers, and at night by crowds of all ages and both sexes seeking entertainment, so that "deviant" behavior and dress is more tolerated there than in the center of the city. *Hijab al-hob*'s men, on the other hand, are shown walking and chatting day and night, in the streets of Casablanca.

One way to facilitate women's presence in public spaces, in the film as in the reality for Moroccan women, is with the car, which is transformed into yet another layer of veiling that mediates between women's bodies and the streets. Cars are increasingly important for women, particularly in large urban centers. The availability of loans has made it easier for them to acquire one, resulting in an increase in automobile purchases by women. [44] Similarly, the car in *Hijab al-hob* plays an important role in the quotidian life of the film's women. A car is more than just a means for them to travel safely through men's public domains, particularly at night. It cloisters the women as they move from one indoor space to another. At times, it even operates as an alternative to the home. This is especially important for unmarried women such as Batoul and her friends. Some of the most intimate exchanges between Batoul and Hamza take place in the car, not because they are audacious or because it is sexually arousing, but simply because finding a place for intimacy between unmarried consenting adults is difficult, not to mention illegal. Article 490 of the Moroccan constitution punishes sexual relationships outside marriage between consenting adults of the opposite sex by one month to one year of prison, while article 489 punishes "unnatural" sexual relationships between consenting adults of the same sex by six months to three years of prison, plus a fine. However, such moments of intimacy inside the car between Batoul and Hamza are short lived. A guard soon finds them kissing and chases them away with insults. Their display of affection, however, could have had more serious consequences. In addition to article 490, the morality police may intervene at any time to inquire about the nature of a man and a woman's relationship. Although in such cases both women and men are targeted, these persecutions almost always aim at humiliating women. This is well documented in an essay by Fedwa Msik entitled "Qui me protège de la police?" (Who Will Protect Me from the Police?) Msik describes how an evening with friends turns into a nightmare of insults when the police stop her and her (male) friend who was giving her a ride home. Their only crime was that they live close to one another and thought it would be convenient for them to travel in the same car.[45] In this context, it is ironic that women in Saudi Arabia are fighting for the right to drive, assuming that driving would give them freedom. While it would certainly allow them to become more productive and less dependent on a male relative or driver to accompany them, driving in the Muslim world does not necessarily translate into freedom. Even when they own and drive cars, women are not welcomed in public space.

While women have found various ways to respond to this unwelcomeness, many make the obvious choice and stay indoors. This is particularly evident in *Hijab al-hob*, in which most of the scenes are set indoors: Batoul's home, the hospital where she works, restaurants, nightclubs, the *hammam* (public bath), and Hamza's apartment. To exaggerate the claustrophobic effect of being *inside*, the interior spaces depicted in the film are often without windows, an absence which is compensated for with artificial lights and an accumulation of objects. It is inside these spaces that women feel safe enough to remove their many veils in order to make confessions to one another and talk without fear about love, sex, adultery, and insecurities. An optimistic feminist is likely to celebrate the liberties that women enjoy in such enclosed, sometimes segregated spaces like the *hammam* as examples of women's empowerment in the community of women. However, the constant need to find the silver lining even in unjust situations blinds feminists like Wolf to the reasons why educated, independent women feel compelled to cover their bodies just to be "free" in the streets. Resistance is not about succumbing to deep patriarchal anxieties about women's bodies by covering them. Indeed, Marnia Lazreg audaciously calls on women *not* to wear the veil: "It is up to women today to make the next step and put an end to the politics of the veil by simply not wearing it as many women did in the 1950s and 1960s. It is women's obligation to history to forge ahead as agents of social change and complete the work started by the previous generations."[46] Lazreg's daring statement arises from her personal concerns. As an Algerian woman she has witnessed how Islamist revival impacts women. During the civil war in Algeria, several thousand Algerian girls and women were abducted or murdered by emerging Islamist groups in their retaliation against the secular government.[47] It stands to reason that, of all feminists with a Muslim background, Algerian and Iranian feminists are least likely to be optimistic about compatibility between religious doctrine and women's rights. They know firsthand that political empowerment of Islamists has detrimental consequences for the status of women. One would expect Wolf and other feminists in the West to lend their support to these feminists as they fight against injustice and orthodoxy.

In Wolf's defense, however, at least she addressed the issue of the veil. Many feminists today refuse to comment on the veil, insisting that it is a woman's choice to dress as she pleases, and that it is a distraction from "important issues." As this chapter has shown, however, the question of "choice" is not a simple one, since women often find themselves coerced into "choosing" the veil through societal pressures or even violence. It is important to maintain a dialogue about the veil because it affects how women are perceived and the place they construct for themselves in society. It also affects how women experience their citizenship as equal to men in terms of responsibility, but unequal regarding their rights, including the right to enjoy the streets they themselves financed as taxpayers. More importantly, in the wake of the Arab Spring, questions about Muslim women, the veil, and their citizenship are as important as any other issues on the table. As Islamist governments take political control of most North African nations, now is the time to examine, as chapter 5 does, the impact of Islamic democracy on women. Will an Islamic democracy protect women's right to walk or drive, accompanied or unaccompanied, with or without a purpose?

NOTES

1. Katherine Bullock, *Rethinking Muslim Women and the Veil: Challenging Historical and Modern Stereotypes* (Herndon: International Institute of Islamic Thought, 2002), 183.

2. "Liberation by the Veil," available at http://www.al islam.org/about/contributions/liberationbytheveil.html (25 November 2012).

3. Madeleine Bunting, "Can Islam Liberate Women? Muslim Women and Scholars Think it Does—Spiritually and Sexually," *The Guardian* 7 December 2001, available at http://www.guardian.co.uk/education/2001/dec/08/socialsciences.highereducation (25 November 2012).

4. See Lila Abu-Lughod, "Do Muslim Women Really Need Saving? Anthropological reflections on Cultural Relativism and Its Others," *American Anthropologist* 104 (2002): 783–90.

5. Naomi Wolf, *The Beauty Myth: How Images of Beauty Are Used Against Women* (New York: Doubleday, 1991), 290.

6. For example, see Sara Buys, "Muslim Women: Beneath the Veil," *The Independent* 29 October 2006, available at http://www.independent.co.uk/news/uk/this-britain/muslin-women-beneath-the-veil-421736.html (25 November 2012); Jesse Sposato, "Conservative Muslim Women Hide Knack for Fashion Under their Religious Robes," *The New York Sun*, 27 January 2008, available at http://www.nysun.com/national/conservative-muslim-women-hide-knack-for-fashion/70250/ (25 November 2012).

7. Naomi Wolf, "Behind the Veil Lives a Thriving Muslim Sexuality," *The Sydney Morning Herald* 30 August 2008, available at http://www.smh.com.au/news/opinion/behind-the-veil-lives-a-thriving-muslim-sexuality/2008/08/29/1219516734637.html (25 November 2012).

8. Marnia Lazreg, *Questioning the Veil: Open Letters to Muslim Women* (Princeton: Princeton University Press, 2009), 7.

9. Helen Razer, "At Least Women in Burqas Are Not Judged on Their Looks," *The Sydney Morning Herald* 18 September 2009, available at http://www.smh.com.au/opinion/at-least-women-in-burqas-are-not-judged-on-their-looks-20090918-fuwc.html (25 November 2012).

10. Bunting, "Can Islam Liberate Women?"

11. Neha Tara Mehta, "Bikini a Disfiguring Garment: Germaine Greer," *India Today* 20 March 2011, available at http://indiatoday.intoday.in/story/india-today-conclave-2011-bikini-a-disfiguring-garment-germaine-greer/1/132925.html (25 November 2012).

12. Anorexia, for example, is increasingly an issue throughout Muslim countries. Although specific rates for eating disorders are not available, online publications indicate higher trends in eating disorders, especially among younger women. For example, for the specific case of Morocco, see "L'anorexie, un sujet tabou," *Lalati* 10 April 2012, available at http://www.lalati.ma/fr/marocaines/l%E2%80%99anorexie-sujet-tabou-16634 (25 November 2012).

13. The official website can be accessed at http://www.sportplazza.com/ (25 November 2012).

14. For example, see the Facebook pages for Lady Fitness, a chain of 25 gyms throughout Morocco.

15. In Morocco, the most popular procedures in order of cost are hair transplant and rhinoplasty, being the most expensive, followed by phalloplasty, otoplasty, and liposuction being the least costly. For more, refer to the investigation conducted by the French-language Moroccan weekly magazine *TelQuel*, available at http://www.telquel-online.com/332/maroc4_332.shtml (25 November 2012).

16. The official website can be accessed at http://www.ibnbattutamall.com/ (25 November 2012).

17. The official website can be accessed at http://www.moroccomall.net/index.html (25 November 2012).

18. The blog "YOU ARE THE STYLE" can be accessed athttp://youarethestyle.blogspot.com/(25 November 2012).

19. Anne-Sophie Martin, "Diamantine: 216,000 foulards et djellabas vendus par an," *La VIEeco* 28 Juin 2011, available at http://www.lavieeco.com/news/histoire-des-marques-au-maroc/diamantine-216-000-foulards-et-djellabas-vendus-par-an-19836.html (25 November 2012).

20. Numerous YouTube channels are dedicated exclusively to the fashionable ways of wearing the veil. Tutorials reach hundreds of thousands of viewers. See for example the channel of the woman whose username is Amenakin (http://www.youtube.com/user/Amenakin) (25 November 2012).

21. Naomi Wolf, "Behind the Veil Lives a Thriving Muslim Sexuality."

22. Trends in sex searches, as well as the most common words used for such searches, are constantly changing. For more, see http://www.google.com/trends/

23. It is important to note that not all searches containing sex are necessarily pornographic searches, as titles of films such as *Sex and the City* or searches for Vatican sex scandals are also included in the statistics. It is not possible to distinguish the pornographic searches from others.

24. *Hijab al-hob* (Amours voilées),), dir. Aziz Salmy (Les Films de C Cléopâtre,, 2008).

25. "Cinema: Zemzemi veut la peau de Aziz Salmy," *La Gazette du Maroc* 16 January 2009, available at http://www.lagazettedumaroc.com/articles.php?id_artl=19191 (25 November 2012).

26. Meriama Moutik, "Polemique: La culture selon le PJD," *TelQuel [Online]*, December 2001, available at http://www.telquel-online.com/archives/501/mage_culture1_501.shtml (25 November 2012).

27. Djamila Gerard, *Amours voil é es* et le député Islamiste marocain," *Riposte laique* 2 Mars 2009, available at http://ripostelaique.com/La-femme-voilee-vue-par-un-depute.html.

28. Sid Ahmed Hammouche, "Scandale au Maroc: un cineaste leve le voile sur l'amour," *Rue89* 26 March 2009, available at http://www.rue89.com/2009/03/26/scandale-au-maroc-un-cineaste-leve-le-voile-sur-lamour (26 November 2012).

29. Ibid., translation from French is mine.

30. The term "ninja" is commonly used in Morocco to refer to women covered in a black niqab.

31. Amina Sadiqi, *Women, Gender, and Language in Morocco* (Leiden: Brill, 2003), 201.

32. Youssef Ziraoui, "Amours et voiles sont compatibles," *TelQuel [Online]*, available at http://www.telquel-online.com/360/interrogatoire_360.shtml (26 November 2012).

33. Nermeen Shaikh, "Why We Can't Save Afghan Women: Interview with Lila Abu-Lughod," *Asia Society*, available at http://asiasociety.org/policy/social-issues/women-and-gender/why-we-cant-save-afghan-women?page=0,1 (26 November 2012).

34. Bullock, *Rethinking Muslim Women and the Veil*, 103.

35. For the case of Iran for example, see Majid Mohammadi, "Harassment and Abuse in Iran: Women Viewed as Sex Objects in Shari'a and Customary Law," *A Forum on Human Rights and Democracy in Iran,* 9 March 2009, available at http://www.gozaar.org/english/articles-en/Harassment-and-Abuse-in-Iran.html (26 November 2012).

36. Moroccan artist Rachid Jadir created a series of animations around the concept of "Rass Derb" that can be accessed on YouTube and Facebook.

37. Moriane Morellec, "Sanhadja Akrouf: 'On est le relai des femmes qui se battent en Algerie," *Modomix* 3 July 2012, available at http://www.mondomix.com/fr/news/sanhadja-akrouf-est-le-relai-des-femmes-qui-se-battent-en-algerie (26 November 2012).

38. Samir Haddadi, "Setif: deux étudiantes agressées pour ne pas avoir porte le voile," *Tout Sur L'Algerie* 2 December 2011, available at http://www.bivouac-id.com/billets/tolerance-islamique-en-algerie-deux-etudiantes-agressees-pour-ne-pas-avoir-porte-le-voile/ (26 November 2012).

39. Fatiha Nakhli, "Tiznit: moul pekala encore en cavale," *L'Economiste* 13 August 2012, available at http://www.leconomiste.com/article/897582-tiznit-moul-pekala-encore-en-cavale (26 November 2012).

40. "15 girls die as zealots 'drive them into blaze,'" *The Telegraph* 15 March 2002, available athttp://www.telegraph.co.uk/news/worldnews/middleeast/saudiarabia/1387874/15-girls-die-as-zealots-drive-them-into-blaze.html(26 November 2012).

41. "Saudi women with attractive eyes may be forced to cover them up, if resolution is passed," *Daily Mail* 18 November 2011, available athttp://www.dailymail.co.uk/news/article-2063143/Saudi-women-attractive-eyes-forced-cover-resolution-passed.html(26 November 2012).

42. "Breastfeeding fatwa causes stir," *BBC News* 22 May 2007, available at http://news.bbc.co.uk/2/hi/6681511.stm (26 November 2012).

43. Translation from Moroccan Arabic to English is mine. The song was made available online in 2006. An interview with the group as well as links to their songs, including "7ijab Style," are available at http://rapdumaroc.skyrock.com/1103751480-SlaM-d-AlLaH.html (26 November 2012).

44. Moroccan daily *Le Matin* published an article about the difference between Moroccan women and men when it comes to purchasing a vehicle. It is interesting to see the difference in male and female behavior when it comes to purchasing cars in Morocco. See Badr Bentak "Les femmes au Volant: les automobilistes sont majoritairement des femmes jeunes et actives," *Le Matin* 8 August 2008, available at http://www.lematin.ma/Actualite/Express/ArticlePrint.asp?id=96261 (26 November 2012).

45. Fedwa Msik, "Qui me protège de la police?" *Qandisha* 17 April 2012, available at http://www.qandisha.ma/2012/04/17/qui-me-protege-de-la-police/ (26 November 2012).

46. Lazreg, *Questioning the Veil*, 101.

47. Youssef M. Ibrahim, "As Algerian Civil War Drags On, Atrocities Grow," *New York Times* 28 December 1997, available athttp://www.nytimes.com/1997/12/28/world/as-algerian-civil-war-drags-on-atrocities-grow.html?pagewanted=all&src=pm(26 November 2012).

FIVE

The Fallen Queens of Islam

How the Arab Revolutions Are Failing Women

Feminist work in Islamic societies is often considered secondary to more important issues. Instead of isolating women's rights and calling for a movement to further them, observers often counter that promoting democracy will eventually lead to advancement for men and women alike. The recent uprisings in North Africa, however, reveal that a quest for democracy does not necessarily entail a concern with achieving equality between women and men. In a matter of months, governments elected by the people replaced three longstanding North African presidents who were removed from office one after the other: first, Tunisia's Zine El Abidine Ben Ali on January 14, 2011, then Egypt's Hosni Mubarak on February 11, and finally Muammar al-Gaddafi of Libya on October 20.

This "fall of dictators" has been celebrated everywhere as the well-deserved victory of oppressed youth over an aging ruling elite. Since the beginning of the uprisings, aware of the West's "concern" for Muslim women, Arabic-language newspapers and television stations made it a point to emphasize women's presence among the crowds in Tunisian streets and in Cairo's Tahrir Square. In anticipation of Western critique, al-Jazeera and other Arab television networks strategically displayed, almost obsessively, images of mostly veiled women marching, chanting, and being arrested by police in order to highlight women's participation in these uprisings. A close examination of less "official" sources, including blogs, YouTube videos, and Facebook pages tells a different story. These digital narratives show that at the center of these uprisings is a yearning to exorcise an authoritative feminine in order to recuperate a *rujula*, or manhood, of which young Tunisians, Egyptians, and Libyans feel that they have been robbed. This chapter examines the place of masculinity and femininity in the discourse of these so-called revolutions. I argue that although the dictators might have left office, the androcentric mentality that allowed them to rule with an iron fist continues to disable half of the youth in these countries: the women.

The first section of this chapter focuses on the representations of the "queens" of the uprisings. Women such as Leila Trabelsi and Suzanne Mubarak came to occupy center stage in the narratives of Arab uprisings as demonized figures that represent the ills of their societies. In order to restore the nation's *natural* hegemonic patriarchal order, these women had to be exposed and expelled. The second part of the chapter turns to the notion of *rujula* and the violent methods through which it is reaffirmed in the wake of the uprisings. Anxiety over masculinity, this section will assert, is a testimony to these uprisings' inability to accomplish any meaningful political and social reforms. The last section examines the status of women in these countries after the uprisings.

THE FALLEN QUEENS OF THE "REVOLUTION"

As events in the Arab world unfolded, a number of powerful but despised women emerged. Newspapers inside and outside the Arabo-Muslim world have been dominated by the figure of Leila Trabelsi, wife of former Tunisian dictator, Ben Ali. To the Spaniards she was "la jefa de la orquesta," as *El País* calls her,[1] while in French publications she became known as "la régente de Carthage," using the title of her unauthorized French biography, first published in 2009.[2] Similarly, in Arabic-language newspapers she has been described as manipulative, power-hungry and a gold-digger.[3] She was said to be the head of her "clan," for which she secured a monopoly over many of the country's industries. According to these accounts, she rose from humble beginnings as a simple hairdresser to become the most powerful woman in Tunisia, rendering her husband impotent long before the street removed him from office. It was reported by news agencies that she escaped from Tunisia to Saudi Arabia with $50 million worth of gold, which will secure her the same extravagant lifestyle, even in exile.[4]

Similarly, though to a far lesser extent, Suzanne Mubarak became the object of attacks from different sides. Egyptian feminists, such as Nawal El Saadawi, accused her of "kill[ing] the feminist movement."[5] Her husband, Hosni Mubarak, blamed her for his downfall.[6] Egyptian citizens, both women and men, held her responsible for the country's many political and economic problems. She was believed to be the one with the political power, while Mubarak was merely a puppet who executed her orders. Long before the revolution, protesters had chanted in Egyptian streets: "Suzanne ya Suzanne, libis Mubarak il-fustan" (Suzanne, hey Suzanne, [Hosni] Mubarak has put on a dress).

Another controversial first lady who gained center stage in the Arabo-Muslim world in the wake of the revolutions was the wife of King Abdullah II of Jordan, Queen Rania, a woman of Palestinian origin. Her lavish lifestyle, which is widely documented online through pictures and You-Tube videos that catch her shopping in Saint Tropez, socializing with the jet set, and sitting front row at Paris fashion shows, has made her an international celebrity, adored in the West and despised in a conservative-leaning Jordanian society. In addition to her visibility, she has been criticized by the country's tribes for promoting the interests of Palestinians over Jordanians. Finally, in early February 2011, as the events in Egypt were unfolding, 36 tribal leaders sent a statement to King Abdullah II explaining that "Before stability and food, the Jordanian people seek liberty, dignity, democracy, justice, equality, human rights and an end to corruption." By "corruption" they are specifically referring to Queen Rania, who, like Leila and Suzanne, has also been accused of nepotism and meddling in her husband's political work. While the signatories were not critical of the king himself, they threatened a "crisis of authority" similar to the ones in Tunisia and Egypt, unless he put an end to his wife's "interference" in the country's political matters.[7]

It is undeniable that these Arab "queens" have been complicit in regimes that oppressed both men and women, though their degree of culpability may vary. While to the West these "queens" have long represented the face of an emancipated woman whose liberation is compatible with Islamic values, the reality is that their efforts to promote women's rights did not result in any significant reforms or improve women's status in their countries. For example, as Nesrine Malik has pointed out, while Queen Rania came to be known as an advocate for Muslim women, which earned her invitations to appear on *Oprah* and other television talk shows, Jordan "still has the highest incidence of honor killings in the Arab world."[8] Similarly, it has been argued that while Leila Trabelsi "verbally champion[ed] women's causes," her preoccupation with financial gain hindered rather than furthered the feminist cause in Tunisia.[9]

These women have been isolated to symbolize all that is wrong with their husbands' repressive regimes. While the uprisings are against male dictators, their queens came to represent illegitimate authority. In the popular narratives, from the media to the streets, it was believed that they used their sexual power to lure prominent men. According to this narrative, they eventually succeeded in taking charge of the state and its wealth, while reducing their husbands to impotent puppets. Ironically, these women have been demonized to the extent that their husbands the dictators, in comparison, seem benign. The last exchange between Leila Trabelsi and Ben Ali before they escaped from Tunisia constructs Ben Ali as powerless and feminine in the face of Leila's masculine firmness. Refusing to board the plane, he supposedly said to her: "I don't want to go. I want to die in my country." Having neither time nor patience for Ben

Ali's capricious patriotism, she firmly responds: "All my life I've had to put up with your stupidity. Just get on!"[10] One almost feels pity for a repenting child-like Ben Ali. Like father figures who have long underestimated the true worth of their sons, the dictators finally wake up, albeit too late, from the spell under which their wives have put them.

The rebelling youth, too, found it necessary to liberate themselves from the manipulative queens, which they achieved through a narrative that vilified these women. Hence the anxiety over Leila, Rania, and Suzanne's power and corruption goes beyond a quest for justice. It announces the misogynist ambitions of a romanticized notion of masculinity that can be achieved only after exorcizing the feminine, thereby avenging the Oedipal killing of a feminized and infantilized father. Only then will "true" men, or *rjal*, emerge. Unlike their dethroned fathers, the new male political subjects will not relinquish leadership to women.

THE *RJAL* OF THE "REVOLUTION"

The rhetoric of these revolutions certainly has misogynistic overtones; restoring *rujula* has been one of the primary goals of the uprisings. One heard repeated references to revolution as the work of *real men*, with Mohamed Bouazizi (1984–2011), whose self-immolation triggered the so-called Arab Spring, as the epitome of manhood. As a commentator on one of the YouTube videos dedicated to Bouazizi's heroism stated: "Mohammed Bouazizi un HOMME UN VRAI [*sic*]" (Mohammed Bouazizi, a true man.)[11] In fact, the so-called revolution in Tunisia was initiated by Bouazizi's attempt to reaffirm his *rujula* (manhood) after being slapped by Fadila Hamdi, a woman police officer. Hamdi's violent act is believed to be a reaction to Bouazizi's own verbal sexual violence. Accounts relate that, after she confiscated the weights he used to price fruits, Bouazizi asked if he should now weigh his fruits using her breasts. Challenged by a woman's display of power, Bouazizi's only defense against such humiliation was to impose his masculinity by reminding her of her breasts, which, although hidden behind a police uniform, still "betray" her womanhood, a condition that necessarily should make her inferior to him in the patriarchal order. Her own use of physical violence in turn insults his *karama* (dignity) leaving him no option to regain his honor other than, as one of his cousins put it, to commit suicide, "or to kill the woman."[12]

Rather than question a culture in which being humiliated by a woman is worse than a slow and painful death, the question following the fall of Ben Ali was whether Egyptians, Libyans, Algerians, Jordanians and other Arab Muslims are *rjal* (men) enough to do what Tunisians had done. The Egyptian journalist Abdel-Halim Qandil stated that "Egypt needs a man like Mohamed Bouazizi."[13] Indeed, the Egyptian riots were often seen as fruitful unrest carried out by *abna' misr* (sons of Egypt) while *banat misr* (daughters of Egypt) are not even considered. On al-Jazeera's Facebook page a commentator wrote, *"lybiya el athima . . . yelzemha rajel athim . . . wliybiya kolha rjal"* (Libya the great . . . needs a great man . . . and all of Libya is men).[14] Hence, while the revolutionaries sought to create an inclusive movement that brought together people of all ages, genders, and socioeconomic backgrounds, they did so by recurring to a male chauvinist discourse that constructed masculinity and men as the only agents of power.

Such discourse about masculinity is ironically a continuation of the language and practices of the dictators and their regimes. The dictatorships of Ben Ali, Mubarak, el-Qaddafi and others sought to strip men of their *rujula* as a way of punishing them for their critique of their regimes. For example, it has been reported that Libyan President Muammar al-Gaddafi had women soldiers torture and execute politically subversive men because, in the context the Arab patriarchal society, humiliation by a woman is far greater than if it were carried out by a man.[15] Human rights violations in the prisons of Ben Ali and Mubarak, often using rape or threats of rape to punish political dissidents, are well documented.[16] This state-sponsored torture sought to reduce men to a condition of subordination usually occupied by women in patriarchal societies since torture of a sexual nature further feminizes the body of the enemy through penetration. As Diana Taylor puts it, the one being tortured is feminized as the "receptive" while the one committing the act of torture reaffirms his masculinity as the "insertive." The torturer's "heterosexuality" remains intact since in the context of his culture's masculinist ideology, as a "top" he still adheres to heteronormative ideals of sexual interaction.[17] Beyond the individual relationship, however, such gendering of torture seeks to establish the state, through its police and military, as powerful and masculine, while feminizing and subjugating the state's enemies.

Dictators and their regimes also used political dissenters' women relatives to further humiliate them. Rape of women was often used as a strategy of degrading not only the woman, but more often, her husband, brother, or father. In Mubarak's prisons, sexual violence against women was at times used as a tactic to obtain confessions from men.[18] Ben Ali's police routinely raped women to punish their dissenting male relatives and deter other men from potential transgressions. This was particularly the case during the uprising in Tunisia, as Sihem Bensedrine, head of the National Council for Civil Liberties, testified: "In poor areas, women who had nothing to do with anything, were raped in front of their families. Guns held back the men; the women were raped in front of them."[19] To an even greater extent, al-Gaddafi ordered his police to use sexual violence against women in order to punish rebelling men. In fact, because of the numerous rape cases, the International Criminal Court investigated the Libyan president's use of rape as a weapon of war.[20]

Nevertheless, what is often silenced in discussions of rape in the context of political and military conflicts is that sexual violence against women can be effective only if both parties regard women as the guardians of men's honor rather than as free agents. Rape in this instance transforms the woman's body into the site of a violent transaction between men. As scholars of violence have argued, rape, both in times of peace but especially in times of war, is violence not only against the individual body but also, and more importantly, against the supposed male guardian and "owner" of the woman's body.[21] One man dishonors another by sexually penetrating the body of his enemy's woman. Naji Barakat, Libya's interim health minister, illustrates this point best: "I think the tactic of Gadhafi is always to try to humiliate Libyans. One thing he knows, the dignity of women is very important to men... He wants to humiliate them even more by having mercenaries do it [. . .]. It is a very dirty tactic."[22] Rather than point to the traumatic effect of rape on the women victims, Barakat seems to be more concerned about how Gaddafi's rape of women affects men, thus becoming complicit in the rape of the same women he defends. Rape as a military tactic results from the conspiracy between men on both sides of the conflict. This attitude dates back to premodern times as discussed in the case of the *morilla* in chapter 2.

While old dictators and "young" revolutionaries may find themselves on opposite sides of the political divide, they concur as to their duty to defend *their* women's honor, chastity, and virginity. Sexist and paternalistic notions that link a man's value and reputation to his ability to monitor and control women's sexual behavior ultimately leave women vulnerable and exposed to sexual aggression from any "revolutionary" man who seeks to retaliate against the woman's father, brother, or husband. Consequently, women relatives of men who were in favor of dictators' regimes were also raped by the revolutionaries. This was particularly the case in Libya, where rebels were accused of raping women, including Nigerian and other sub-Saharan girls and women, to punish their male relatives for fighting on the side of Gaddafi.[23]

Male Gaddafi loyalists, too, endured torture, mutilation, and the humiliation previously reserved for critics of the regime. It was the rebels' turn to reaffirm their *rujula* through violence against a feminized enemy. Gaddafi and his son were eventually killed and stripped naked, made to assume a feminized position penetrated, as it were, by the gaze of Libyan citizens. Videos even show Gaddafi being sodomized upon his capture by one of the rebels.[24] Hence by insisting obsessively on reclaiming their *rujula*, the so-called revolutionaries merely reinforce already established hierarchical binary oppositions such as the masculine/feminine. Beyond the implications such notions hold for the role of women in "post-dictatorship" Tunisia, Egypt, and Libya, one can't help but be skeptical of the political and social reforms that will be carried out by long-oppressed men with a new found confidence in their *rujula*.

   Much has been written about these so-called revolutions, both inside and outside the Arab world, most of it in celebratory tones. Journalists, bloggers, YouTubers, Twitterers, and intellectuals have praised the upheavals as a "turning point" in Arab countries. The obsession with "turning points" says much about a culture that is fascinated with the performance of change but refuses to leave the comfort of the familiar. The "Jasmine," "*ful*," and other so-called revolutions might have been facilitated by twenty-first century technologies (Twitter, Facebook, YouTube, blogs, etc.), but the rhetoric is not new, nor is it unique. *L'événement déclencheur* was one man's attempt to recuperate his *rujula* after a woman supposedly humiliated him in public. Other Tunisians, Egyptians, and Libyans have followed suit. First they expelled their "queens", then they killed, figuratively or literally, their castrated rulers. As the world watched, these revolutions went on to empower traditionalist Islamist parties. One is left wondering pessimistically what will happen next.

WOMEN AND THE "REVOLUTION" THAT FAILED THEM

During the initial euphoria after the fall of dictators, when skeptics voiced their fears about how the uprisings were going to affect women, such fears were mocked as reminiscent of Orientalist and colonialist mentalities that affirmed the West's superiority to the Muslim world through promoting women's rights. Moreover, skeptics were assumed to be defending the regimes of Ben Ali and Mubarak, whose concern for women's rights, it is often repeated, was solely for political ends. As Reuel Marc Grecht explains:

> Many Americans and Europeans would probably prefer to see secular dictatorships in power in the Arab Middle East that uphold modern Western standards on women's issues than see an Islamic democracy where the social and legal rights women enjoy in the West might be curtailed. They may well understand that dictatorships in the Middle East have done terrible things to their societies, including fertilizing the ground for Bin Ladenism, but they still cannot bring themselves to approve of a political process that could lead to the diminution of women's rights. [25]

Although many scholars, including feminists, have dismissed Westerners' preoccupation with Muslim women's rights, over a year after the so-called revolutions, these fears about the impact of Islamist governments in North Africa are finally being put to the test. Even though the Arab uprisings were not initiated by Islamists, both Tunisia and Egypt elected Islamist governments, making Libya the exception. [26] In the wake of the uprisings, three of the five North African countries officially fell to the control of Islamist parties: the Muslim Brotherhood's newly formed Freedom and Justice Party (FJP) in Egypt, Ennahda in Tunisia, and the Party of Justice and Development (PJD) in Morocco. The outcomes of these countries' democratic elections reveal that concerns about women's rights were justified.

As the first country to overthrow its ruler, thus marking the beginning of the Arab spring, Tunisia was also the first to democratically elect an Islamist party. Ennahda won more than 41% of the vote and secured 90 seats in the 217-member assembly. Although Tunisia's was often called the revolution of youth, it was sixty-two year-old Hamadi Jebali who became Prime Minister in December 2011. In July 2012, seventy one-year-old Rachid Ghannouchi, co-founder of the Ennahda movement, was re-elected to serve as party leader for two more years. In addition to reserving leadership positions in the government for an aging elite, the new government sought to infringe still more on Tunisian women's rights which had been accorded to them by previous governments, some as early as 1956, when President Habib Bourguiba established The Code of Personal Status (CPS). The reforms promulgated by the CPS were revolutionary. It banned polygamy and the veil, and revised laws concerning almost all aspects of family life including marriage, divorce, custody, and adoption. The CPS gave women the right to ask for divorce and took away the husband's right to repudiate his wife;[27] it has been regularly updated since then.[28] Most subsequent amendments were also initiated by the state. In 1988, in one of his earlier speeches, President Ben Ali insisted that "The Code of Personal Status is a gain to which we attach great importance and which we will continue to uphold. We are truly proud of the CPS, and there will be no going back on Tunisia's progress in the domains of family and women's rights."[29] In 1993 a second major wave of reforms secured Tunisian women even more rights, including the right to transmit nationality to their children regardless of the nationality of the father.[30]

In spite of these rights, Tunisian women are still not on equal footing with men. Laws regarding inheritance and marriage to non-Muslims are different for women, relegating more rights to men. Nevertheless, generally speaking, compared to the status of women in most countries in North Africa and the Middle East, Tunisian women fare much better. Since most reforms, particularly the early ones, were initiated by the state rather than by feminist movements, all Tunisians had to comply, whether they agreed or not. Even Islamic fundamentalists such as Rached Ghannouchi, who disagreed with the CPS because it was against Islamic law, had to "tolerate" these laws.[31]

Because they were imposed by the ruling elite, however, the reforms did not coincide with the beliefs of the patriarchal majority. Hence even before the uprising, the fundamentalist movement had been critical of the CPS. As Mounira Charrad has pointed out, in the late 1980s and early 1990s conservative Islamic leaders were already calling for abolishing the CPS, which they viewed as opposing *sharia* (Islamic law). There were calls for revising all the CPS positions vis-à-vis polygamy, divorce, and the equality between women and men.[32]

With this background in mind, it should not come as a surprise that once it secured the majority in parliament, Ennahda sought to revise the CPS to make it conform to Islamic law. This would entail serious changes such as lifting the ban on polygamy and revising laws about the age of marriage.[33] In fact, high-ranking members of Ennahda have already made statements about reinstituting polygamy and customary marriage, though such statements were soon recanted following the outrage they caused.[34] However, the most scandalous setback for Tunisian women came in the draft of the proposed new constitution, in which women are assigned a "complementary" rather than equal status in relation to men. Article 28 of the proposed Tunisian constitution describes women as having a "complementary role inside the family,"[35] rather than one equal to men. Thousands of Tunisian women took to the streets in protest, fearing more injustices if they were to remain silent. Ghannouchi dismissed women's concerns, attributing the confusion to linguistic misunderstanding: "Complementation is an authentic concept, meaning that there would be no man without woman and no woman without man." According to Ghannouchi, "complementation" is "an additional meaning to the meaning of equality."[36]

However, while the media debates what the future holds for Tunisian women, these women are already feeling the impact of the "Islamization" of their country. Muslims in Tunisia, like Muslims everywhere, are often torn between modernity and religious obligations.[37] The findings from focus groups conducted in Tunisia between February 17 and 28, 2012, reveal that Tunisians' attempt to reconcile secularism and religion is increasingly difficult. Participants, both women and men, claim to support gender equality but at the same time categorically reject any law that would contradict *sharia*. It is out of the question, for example, to touch inheritance law.[38] One of the focus group interviewees, a thirty-three-year-old man from Sfax, insists that he would support "equality in everything except for the things mentioned in the religion; they cannot be changed."[39] There are women who also believe that gender equality should be achieved while respecting religion. As a twenty-five-year-old woman from Medenine puts it, "We need full equality; there are those who call for equality in inheritance but I think religion needs to be respected."[40] Women's anxiety over possibly losing the status they had under the government of Ben Ali was exacerbated because many men criticized the previous government, and particularly former first lady Leila Ben Ali, for supposedly giving women privileges over men.[41] Women also expressed greater fear than men of physical insecurity in public spaces and increasing harassment in the workplace. According to the respondents, "before the revolution security forces more effectively protected women from harassment."[42] As a twenty three-year-old woman from Sfax contended, "There is some fear after the revolution, I never used to worry about my personal security now all I think about when I'm outside is to go back home safely."[43] Another twenty five-year-old expressed her fear over what she wears: "If a woman wears a mini skirt in Medenine, her legs might be cut."[44] Yet another woman refers to changes in the public arena: "I used to feel more secure when I go out at 3 a.m.; even if Leila Ben Ali imposed that freedom, I didn't really care. Now a high school kid can bother me." There are women who are indeed content with the changes proposed either formally or informally by the new government. A thirty-one year-old woman from Sfax is in favor of revising the ban on polygamy. As she explains, "I think polygamy should be reinstated; it's better to know that my husband has a second wife with my full knowledge and permission than his having mistresses I don't know about. Plus, we now have a serious problem of spinsterhood."[45] Overall, however, women in Tunisia are not confident about what the future holds for them.

The fear for their liberty that women express at Tunisian demonstrations is not manufactured by a Western or Zionist conspiracy seeking to undermine these new governments.[46] They are the fears of Tunisian women who took to the streets, alongside the men, to overthrow a dictatorship, only to find themselves on the brink of a new tyranny, whose authority over and anxiety about women's bodies is already being felt. It did not take long for the new elite to organize a mass protest, calling for women in Tunisia to be veiled.[47] Just a few months after Tunisia's Islamist government took office, Naserdding Ben Saida, general director of the Arabic-language daily *Attounissia*, was arrested for publishing a photo of German-Tunisian soccer player Sami Khedira with his partially naked girlfriend Lina Gercke. Nabil Karoui, the director of the private television station Nessma TV, was ordered to pay a fine for broadcasting the animated Franco-Iranian film *Persepolis*, an act that was viewed as a violation of Islamic moral values since, among other things, the film includes a drawing of Allah.[48] Less than two months after Tunisia's Islamist government took office, a radical Egyptian cleric known for his anti-Semitic, Anti-West, and misogynist sermons, was invited to Tunisia by Tunisia-based Islamist organizations, most of which were established after the fall of the Ben Ali regime.[49] Most controversial is the cleric's support of Female Genital Mutilation (FGM), which he regards as a form of "cosmetic surgery" whose virtues are "supported by Islamic science."[50] Tunisian rights activists did not remain quiet. They filed a legal complaint against the cleric for inciting hatred and violence against other religions, and for abetting "the undermining of women's physical integrity by advocating female circumcision."[51] In the new Tunisia, however, the new government wants to deprive women even of the right to protest. The Tunisian minister of the interior banned all demonstrations on August 13, 2012, Tunisian Women's Day.[52] Even athletes were affected by the new mood in Tunisia. While other nations were celebrating their athletes for winning medals at the 2012 Olympic Games in London, Tunisian athlete Habiba Ghribi, who won the silver medal in the Women's 3000m Steeplechase final, making her the first Tunisian woman to win an Olympic medal, was attacked for her "revealing" running gear.[53]

The case of Tunisia is yet another reminder that the concerns in the West and in Muslim countries regarding the rise of an Islamist party in Tunisia were valid and not mere fabrications. It is indeed true that women in Tunisia are gradually losing the Bourguiba legacy. The changes proposed have caused a media uproar because women in Tunisia have more to lose than other women in the region because of what they have already achieved. It is due to these very achievements, however, that women in Tunisia are better equipped than their counterparts in North Africa and the Middle East to fight these changes. The literacy rate for women in Tunisia is over 70%, higher than that of Morocco (40%), Algeria (60%), and Egypt (59%). Women in Tunisia make up two-thirds of university students compared with two-fifths in Egypt.[54] Thanks to women's education and the country's secular tradition, women in Tunisia are more likely to stand up to Islamists' attempts to exclude them from the public sphere.

The situation of women in Egypt following the revolution seems gloomier. Even before the election of the Islamist party, women protesters in Tahrir Square were subjected to humiliating "virginity tests", which may be expected in a culture that glorifies virginity. But, women were also harassed and sexually assaulted. In the Square, some male demonstrators called on women to "Go back home and feed your babies!"[55] Just as in Tunisia, women in Egypt were in danger of losing the advances that the previous regime made thanks to the Personal Status Laws (PSL). These laws were dubbed "Suzanne's laws" in reference to First Lady Suzanne Mubarak,[56] and as soon as the Mubarak regime fell, hundreds of Egyptians protested, arguing that the laws harm Egyptian families.[57] Demonstrators particularly opposed reforms to divorce and child custody. Thanks to the amendments introduced under Mubarak, the law granted women the option of no-fault divorce, or *khul'*, which allows them to file in court for divorce without the need for a husbands' or male relatives' permission. Another of "Susanne's laws" increased the period that mothers have custody of their children from nine to fifteen years. [58] Suzanne Mubarak's feminist reforms extended to the participation of women in the country's political life. She introduced a parliament quota system, which sets aside 64 seats for women in the over 500-seat parliament. Post-Mubarak Egypt abolished the quota system. As a result, there were only eight women out of 508 seats, or less than 2%, a substantial decrease from the previous 12 percent.[59] Moreover, the Constitutional Reform Committee, named to draft a new constitution for Egypt, did not include a single woman.[60] Finally, the 35-member cabinet of Egypt's first freely elected president includes only two women, one of whom, Nadia Eskandar Zukhari, is also the only member of cabinet who is a Coptic Christian.

Though things may look dismal for Egyptian women's participation in politics, the state of affairs in the private sphere is even more disconcerting. The Islamist Parliament is discussing the possibility of reducing the age of marriage for girls from 18, as established under Mubarak, to 12. Moreover, although Mubarak banned Female Genital Mutilation (FGM) in 2007 after a twelve-year-old girl bled to death,[61] and in spite of the long struggles of feminists such as Nawal El Saadawi to condemn the practice, soon after the fall of Mubarak's regime the Muslim Brotherhood organized campaigns to circumcise women for a nominal fee through mobile health clinics as part of their community outreach.[62] A prominent member of the Freedom and Justice Party (FJP) spoke against the ban on FGM. She insisted that it "is a personal decision and each woman can decide on her needs. If she needs it, she can go to a doctor." In line with statements by other Islamist fundamentalists, she refers to it as "plastic surgery" that aims at beautification.[63]

On the other side of North Africa, in Morocco, there was no uprising, but the country was affected by the Arab Spring nonetheless. In November 2011, for the first time in the kingdom's history, an Islamist party was elected, taking 107 of the 395 seats.[64] The 30-member cabinet includes only one woman, the Minister of Solidarity, Women, Family and Social Development. Because its transition to an Islamist party was peaceful, the impact of Morocco's new government on women's rights is not attracting as much international attention as have similar developments in Tunisia and Egypt. But the impact is just as detrimental from a feminist perspective. An article published by Slate Afrique entitled "Dix raisons de croire que le Maroc pourrait devenir un émirat islamiste" (Ten reasons to believe that Morocco could become an Islamic emirate) summarizes the achievements of the new government one hundred days after its rise to power. In a little over three months, the Moroccan Islamist government censored the press for misrepresenting Islam; accused foreign tourists of being the source of sin; praised controversial religious figures, one of whom once declared a *fatwa* authorizing the marriage of nine-year-old girls;[65] publicly condemned homosexuality and banned the internationally known dancer Noor from appearing on national television because she is a transsexual woman;[66] banned advertising for gambling; condemned art that "promoted debauchery", which included an attempt to prevent Elton John from performing in Morocco because he supposedly encouraged homosexuality; and refused to address injustices in the Moroccan Penal Code.[67] In response to discussions about marriage age in Morocco, the Minister of Solidarity, Women, Family and Social Development declared that "marriage of underage girls must be subject for discussion . . . because many advanced countries allow girls to marry at the

age of 14." She explained that "the issue of child abuse has been politically exploited by associations, which have greatly harmed Morocco's image abroad." These statements made Moroccan feminist and human
rights activist Khadija Rouissi wonder "What is the government's position on these issues if the minister, who is the only woman in government, is against the exposure of violations against children and wom-
en?" [68] When an imam known for his polemical sermons called for the
killing of a journalist who had stated his support for personal and sexual
freedom on a satellite television channel, an MP from the PJD declared
that "Any sexual act outside marriage is considered an act of debauchery,
a crime." Declarations like these are triggering fear among Moroccan
human rights organizations that view them as "attacks on individual
liberty." [69] These statements also bring to mind what a Libyan feminist
said in response to the announcement of a return to *sharia* law in post-
revolutionary Libya: "We did not slay Goliath so that we now live under
the Inquisition." [70] Judging from the reforms under way in post-Arab
Spring North Africa, it looks as if a comparison to the Inquisition is not
necessarily an exaggeration.

The proponents of these governments, however, will be quick to respond to the skeptics, saying that it is still too early to judge. Indeed, it is
too early to determine with certainty how women will fare as citizens of
the new democracies in the Arab world. By looking back at history, one
can attempt to predict the outcome for women of these so-called revolutions. Let's suppose that these uprisings produce results similar to those
of an earlier uprising: the Iranian revolution. Just like Ennahda, the Muslim Brotherhood, and the PJD, all of which have been stressing in their
official discourse their commitment to women's rights, the leaders of
Iran's Islamist revolution, as well, openly expressed the importance of
women, including the revolution's indebtedness to them. In a speech he
gave on May 16, 1979, on the occasion of Women's Day, Ayatollah Khomeini declared that "A woman is not a thing, but a great human being
who raises and cares for society. Her embrace is the creator of men. She is
the nursemaid of humankind, and the source of the people's compassion
and happiness." In a speech he gave on May 6, 1980, Khomeini publicly
acknowledged Iranian women's role in the revolution: "Our uprising is
indebted to women. Men took the example of the women into the streets.
Women encouraged the men to revolt, and sometimes even led the way.
Woman is a wonderful creature. She possesses fiendish, strong (and)
passionate capabilities." [71] But while women were praised in public
speeches, the new government's traditional Islamic values suffocated
women out of the public sphere. For starters, they reinstated *sharia* law,
which exalts the domestic space as the natural place for women. The
Family Protection Law that Shah Reza Pahlavi had introduced to improve women's status in marriage, divorce, and custody, was abolished.
The Family Protection Law also forbade a man from marrying more than

one wife.[72] While the rhetoric paid lip service to the importance of women in society, gender equality was not a goal. In fact, Ayatollah Khomeini believed in a gender-based division of labor both within the home and outside it. Women were "to marry and bear children," while men are better suited to public functions.[73] Like North African Islamist governments, the Iranian government, too, had a negative attitude toward sexuality, which provided them with an excuse for imposing the veil and sex-based segregation in schools and other institutions.[74] Polygamy and *mut'a* (temporary marriage) were viewed as a solution for "spinsterhood."[75] Since they were believed to be emotional and lacking in intellectual abilities, women were dismissed from decision-making positions such as judgeships. Even after more than thirty years, the Islamist government continues to think of ways to contain women's activities in the public sphere. As of the academic year 2012-13, women in Iran are to be banned from 77 fields of study. In response to this human rights violation, Iranian feminist and Nobel Peace Prize laureate Shirin Ebadi wrote a letter of complaint to UN Secretary-General Ban Ki Moon and UN High Commissioner for Human Rights Navi Pillay in which she explains that decisions such as these are "part of the recent policy of the Islamic Republic, which tries to return women to the private domain inside the home as it cannot tolerate their passionate presence in the public arena." In Iran, women make up 60% of university students, yet these students will not be able to major in management, mining engineering, accounting, pure chemistry, or restoration of historic buildings. All this because, according to a senior Iranian education official, "Some fields are not very suitable for women's nature." [76]

Past revolutions in Muslim countries were not particularly favorable to women, and neither are the current ones. Ironically, in their early days, the upheavals in Iran, just like the ones in North Africa, were celebrated by prominent intellectuals, who, in their excessive zeal to criticize the West, turned a blind eye to the tragedy of Muslim women. Michel Foucault, who went to Iran in 1978-79 to cover the revolution as a journalist, wrote that the Iranian revolution "is perhaps the first great insurrection against global systems, the form of revolt that is most modern and most insane."[77] Similarly, Edward Said saw it as a victory over the West, while downplaying the role of religion: "If Iranian workers, Egyptian students, Palestinian farmers resent the West or the U.S., it is a concrete response to the specific policy injuring them as human beings."[78] It is not surprising that neither Foucault nor Said were concerned about how the revolution was affecting women. Thirty years ago, just as today, the question of women's rights was assumed to be illegitimate in times of crisis. Women are, once again, asked to wait until other, "serious" problems are resolved.

To sum up the "Arab Spring," rulers were forced out of office. Young women and men took to the streets. Slogans were chanted. Many lost their voices and others their lives. Whatever happened, if indeed one wants to call it the "revolution of *real* men," is certainly not a revolution for women. Recent changes, if anything, have further solidified patriarchal oppression of women in a region that is in great need of a true feminist victory. New rulers and their parties may have been elected democratically, but democratic values are not merely about imposing the rule of the new majority. Democratic values are about protecting the rights of all citizens, including those who do not conform to a theologian's idea of a "good" woman. In a piece published online in April 2010 in the first issue of the Arabic-language magazine *Mithly*, Morocco's only gay magazine and one of the few in the Arab world,[79] a contributor under the pseudonym Ghulam Abu Nuwas, literally Abu Nuwas' boy (a reference to the openly gay medieval poet mentioned in the first two chapters), greets women who are "prostitutes, sorcerers, lesbians, atheists, [. . .] masculine, those who speak in loud voices, prisoners, HIV positive, those who wear high heels, friends, those who use and those who are used, the single mothers, the ones who refuse to have children, those who dress provocatively."[80] In sum, these women, whom Ghulam Abu Nuwas makes visible by generously giving them a space in his publication, are the Muslim women often made invisible in larger debates, including feminist debates, about gender, rights, citizenship and revolutions. In the Muslim world, one cannot speak of a revolution for women until women, all women, find a place in their country's political systems and its most coveted, powerful institutions.

NOTES

1. Ignacio Cembrero, "Leila Trabelsi fue la jefa de la orquesta," *El País* 26 January 2011, available at http://elpais.com/diario/2011/01/26/internacional/1295996406_850215.html (28 September 2012).

2. Nicolas Beau and Catherine Graciet, *La régente de Carthage: maine basse sur la Tunisie* (Paris: Découverte, 2009). Similar publications include a book by Loti Ben Chrouda, who worked for the Ben Ali household as a cook. See Lotfti Ben Chrouda and Isabelle Soares Boumalala, *Dans l'onbre de la reine par le majordome des Ben Ali* (Paris: Michel Lafon, 2011).

3. For example, in article published on January 16 2011, the Arabic-language news web portal *Moheet* referred to Leila Trabelsi as "shareekat al-shaytan" (partenar of Satan). See http://www.moheet.com/2011/01/16/شريكة-الشيطان-في-الاستبداد-والفساد-لي (28 September 2012).

4. Kim Willsher, "Leila Trabelsi: The Lady Macbeth of Tunisia," *The Guardian* 18 January 2011, available at http://www.guardian.co.uk/world/2011/jan/18/leila-trabelsi-tunisia-lady-macbeth (28 September 2012).

5. Iman Azzi, "Cairo Leaders: Suzanne Mubarak Held Women Back," *WeNews* 17 February 17, 2011, available at http://www.womensenews.org/story/the-world/110216/cairo-leaders-suzanne-mubarak-held-women-back (28 September 2012).

6. The Muslim Brotherhood's Official English website reported that Mubarak blamed his wife Suzanne and son Gamal for ruining his "history in Egypt." See http://www.ikhwanweb.com/article.php?id=28033 (28 September 2012).

7. Randa Habib, "Jordan Tribes Break Taboo by Targeting Queen," *Agence France-Presse* 9 February 2011, available at http://www.google.com/hostednews/afp/article/ALeqM5hF2bnxbMFqWrESNtwFFzDuHeL6lQ (28 September 2012).

8. Nesrine Malik, "Ice Queens of the Arab World," *The Guardian* 15 February 2011, available at http://www.guardian.co.uk/commentisfree/2011/feb/15/queens-arab-middle-east (28 September 2012).

9. Laurie Brand, Rym Kaki and Joshua Stacher, "First Ladies as Focal Points for Discontent," *Foreign Policy* 16 February 2011, available at http://mideast.foreignpolicy.com/posts/2011/02/16/first_ladies_as_focal_points_for_discontent (15 September 2012).

10. Ian Sparks, "'I'm fed up of your stupidity, get on the plane!' How the Tunisian president's wife nagged him to flee the country," *Daily Mail* 11 February 2011, available athttp://www.dailymail.co.uk/news/article-1355944/Tunisian-presidents-wife-nagged-flee-Im-fed-stupidity.html(15 September 2012).

11. The commentary is posted on YouTube at http://www.youtube.com/watch?v=5Nir6FcXDM8

12. Marc Mahuzier "Le petit marchand qui a seme le printemps arabe," *Ouest France* 16 June 2011, available at http://www.ouest-france.fr/actu/actuDet_-Le-petit-marchand-tunisien-qui-a-seme-le-printemps-arabe-_3639-1836111_actu.Htm?xtor=RSS-4&utm_source=RSS_MVI_ouest-france&utm_medium=RSS&utm_campaign=RSS (15 September 2012).

13. Anthony Shadid, "Joy as Tunisian President Flees Offers Lesson to Arab Leaders, *The New York Times* 14 January 2011, available at http://www.nytimes.com/2011/01/15/world/africa/15region.html (12 September 2012).

14. Comments can be viewed on Aljazeera's Facebook page:http://www.facebook.com/aljazeeramubasher/posts/222340017778740 (28 September 2012).

15. Robert Worth, " The Surreal Ruins of Never-Never Land," *The New York Times [online]* 21 September 2011, available at http://www.nytimes.com/2011/09/25/magazine/the-surreal-ruins-of-qaddafis-never-never-land.html?pagewanted=8&hpw (28 September 2012).

16. See Jean Allain, *International Law in the Middle East: Closer to Power than Justice* (Burlington: Ashgate, 2004) and Basma Abdel Aziz, "Torture in Egypt," *Torture* 17 (2007).

17. Diana Taylor, *Disappearing Acts: Spectacles of Gender and Nationalism in Argentina's Dirty War* (Durham: Duke University Press, 1997), 155.

18. Basma Abdel Aziz, "Torture in Egypt," 50.

19. Angelique Chrisafis, "Confusion, Fear and Horror in Tunisia as Old Regime's Militia Carries on the Fight," *The Guardian* 16 January 2011, available at http://www.guardian.co.uk/world/2011/jan/16/tunisia-gun-battle-army-tunis (27 September 2012).

20. Elizabeth Flock, "Gaddafi Ordered Mass Rapes in Libya, ICC Prosecutor Says," *The Washington Post* 9 June 2011, available at http://www.washingtonpost.com/blogs/blogpost/post/gaddafi-ordered-mass-rapes-in-libya-icc-prosecutor-says/2011/06/09/AG1D0TNH_blog.html (27 September 2012).

21. See Nancy Scheper-Hughes and Philip Bourgois eds., Violence in War and Peace: An Anthology (Malden: Blackwell University Press, 2004,) especially the volume's introduction.

22. Lara Setrakian, "Libyan Dictator Gadhafi Ordered Rapes to 'Humiliate' His Enemies," *ABC News* 9 June 2011, available at http://abcnews.go.com/International/gadhafi-rape-attacks-meant-humiliate-enemies/story?id=13801507#.UD_5KMhWrx0

23. Evan Hill, "Migrants in Libya Camp Claim Rape," *Aljazeera* 29 August 2011, available at http://www.aljazeera.com/news/africa/2011/08/201182921437789463.html

24. The video is available online at *GlobalPost* 24 October 2011, available at http://www.globalpost.com/dispatch/news/regions/middle-east/111024/gaddafi-sodomized-video-gaddafi   sodomy?page=2&fb_comment_id=fbc_10150346996354051_19199106_10150347187739051 (27 September 2012).

25. Reuel Marc Gerecht *The Wave: Man, God, and the Ballot Box in the Middle East* (Stanford: Hoover Institution Press Publication, 2011), 114.

26. David Kirkpatrick, "Election Results in Libya Break an Islamist Wave," 8 July 2012, available at http://www.nytimes.com/2012/07/09/world/africa/libya-election-latest-results.html?pagewanted=all (27 September 2012).

27. Mounira Charrad, *States and Women's Rights: The Making of Postcolonial Tunisia, Algeria, and Morocco* (Berkeley: University of California Press, 2001), 219.

28. Kristine Goulding, "Tunisia: Women's Winter of Discontent," *Open Democracy* 25 October 2011, available at http://www.opendemocracy.net/5050/kristine-goulding/tunisia-womens-winter-of-discontent (27 September 2012).

29. Quoted in Mounira Charrad and Allyson Goeken, "Continuity or Change: Family Law and Family Structure in Tunisia," *African Families at the Turn of the 21st Century*, ed. Yaw Oheneba-Sakyi and Baffour K. Tayki (Westport: Praeger/Greenwood, 2006), 38.

30. As in most Muslim countries, citizenship was only passed through fathers. See Mounira Charrad, "From Nationalism to Feminism: Family Law in Tunisia," *Family in the Middle East: Ideational Change in Egypt, Iran and Tunisia*, ed. Kathryn Yount and Hoda Rashad (New York: Routledge, 2008), 74.

31. Mounira Charrad, "From Nationalism to Feminism: Family Law in Tunisia," *Family in the Middle East: Ideational Change in Egypt, Iran and Tunisia*, ed. Kathryn Yount and Hoda Rashad (New York: Routledge, 2008), 126.

32. Ibid.,126.

33. "Thousands of Tunisians Want Application of Sharia," *Agence France-Presse* 16 March 2012, available at http://www.google.com/hostednews/afp/article/ALeqM5jWSW6bAMLZhQ4_cBUmTjmtRNTv_g?docId=CNG.8717d4d14cf2a53356bd89267ef74352.211 (27 September 2012).

34. Naji Kheshnawi and Sundus Zarouki, "Tunisia: Shaking the Foundations of Secularism," *Alakhbar* 3 March 2012, available at http://english.al-akhbar.com/node/4771 (27 September 2012).

35. Monica Marks, "'Complementary' Status for Tunisian Women," *Foreign Policy* 20 August 2012, available at http://mideast.foreignpolicy.com/posts/2012/08/20/complementary_status_for_tunisian_women (15 October 2012).

36. Monia Ghanmi, "Tunisian Women March for their Rights," *Maghrebia* 15August 2012, available at http://www.magharebia.com/cocoon /awi/xhtml1/en_GB/features/awi/features /2012/08/15/feature-02 (15 October 2012).

37. A case in point is the controversy surrounding the documentary *Ni Allah, ni Maître* (Neither Allah, nor Master) by Franco-Tunisian filmmaker Nadia El Fani.

38. Gabriella Borovsky and Ama Ben Yahia, "Women's Political Participation in Tunisia After the Revolution: Findings From Focus Groups in Tunisia Conducted February 17-28, 2012," *National Democratic Institute* May 2012, 7, available at http://www.ndi.org/files/womens-political-participation-Tunisia-FG-2012-ENG.pdf (15 October 2012).

39. Ibid., 15.

40. Ibid., 15.

41. Ibid., 14.

42. Ibid., 8.

43. Ibid., 10.

44. Ibid., 14.

45. Ibid., 20.

46. The Muslim Brotherhood's official news outlet, *Ikhwan Online*, is reporting that "the remnants of the dissolved National Democratic Party, the state security apparatus and their Zionist allies" are trying to destabilize Egypt by infiltrating an ongoing sit-in protest in Cairo's Tahrir Square. See http://www.egyptindependent.com/news/brotherhoods-website-alleges-israelis-infiltrating-tahrir-protests (15 October 2012).

47. Hoda Badran "The Arab Spring is Looking Like a Great Leap Backwards for Women," *Europe's World* Summer 2012, available at http://www.europesworld.org/NewEnglish/Home_old/Article/tabid/191/ArticleType/ArticleView/ArticleID/22012/language/en-US/TheArabSpringislookinglikeagreatleapbackwardsforwomen.aspx (15 October 2012).

48. "Tunisia: TV Chief Fined Over a Film," *The New York Times* 4 May 2012, available at http://www.nytimes.com/2012/05/04/world/africa/tunisia-nabil-karoui-fined-over-controversial-film.html (15 October 2012).

49. Wafa Ben Hassine, "Controversial Muslim Cleric from Egypt Visits Tunisia," *Tunisialive* 13 February 2012, available at http://www.tunisia-live.net/2012/02/13/controversial-muslim-cleric-from-egypt-visits-tunisia/ (15 October 2012).

50. Charles Baeder, "Controversial Cleric, Advocate of Female Genital Mutilation, Challenges Tunisian Critics," *Tunisialive* 15 February 2012, available at http://www.tunisia-live.net/2012/02/15/controversial-cleric-advocate-of-female-genital-mutilation-challenges-tunisian-critics/ (15 October 2012).

51. Cecile Feuillatre, "Tunisia Activists File Suit Against Female Circumcision Preacher," *Middle East Online* 15 February 2012, available at http://www.middle-east-online.com/english/?id=50670 (15 October 2012).

52. See report by Gender Concerns International, available athttp://www.genderconcerns.org/article.php?id_nr=3517&id=Tunisian%20Ministry%20of%20the%20Interior%20Bans%20Women's%20Day%20Celebration%20on%20Habib%20Bourguiba%20Avenue

53. Tunisian male swimmer Oussama Mellouli, who won gold in the 10-kilometer marathon and bronze in the 1,500-meter freestyle, did not escape the wrath of the Islamists either. Though he was not criticized for his swimwear, he was attacked for drinking juice before his race during Ramadan. "Tunisian Olympians Targeted by Islamist Radicals for Behavior and Dress Deemed Un-Islamic," *CBS News* 14 August 2012, available at http://www.cbsnews.com/8301-33747_162-57492866/tunisian-olympians-targeted-by-islamist-radicals-for-behavior-and-dress-deemed-un-islamic/ (25 October 2012).

54. "Women and the Arab Awakening: Now is the Time," *The Economist* 25 October 2011, available at http://www.economist.com/node/21532256 (28 October 2012).

55. Sue Lloyd-Roberts, "Has the Revolution Betrayed the Women of Egypt?" *BBC* 13 February 2012, available at http://news.bbc.co.uk/2/hi/programmes/newsnight/9695850.stm (28 October 2012).

56. Hoda Elsadda, "Egypt: The Battle Over Hope and Morale," *Open Democracy* 2 November 2011, available at http://www.opendemocracy.net/5050/hoda-elsadda/egypt-battle-over-hope-and-morale (28 October 2012).

57. Salwa Samir, "Row Over Suzanne Mubarak's Family Law," *The Egyptian Gazette* 29 March 2012, available at http://213.158.162.45/~egyptian/index.php?action=news&id=23604&title=Row%20over%20Suzanne%20Mubarak%E2%80%99s%20family%20law (28 October 2012).

58. Reem Leila, "Controversy Over 'Suzanne's Laws,'" *Al-Ahram* 5–11 May 2011, available at http://weekly.ahram.org.eg/2011/1046/eg14.htm (28 October 2012).

59. Mariz Tadros, "To Empower Women on a Global Scale We Need More than Quotas," *The Guardian* 8 March 2012, available at http://www.guardian.co.uk/global-development/poverty-matters/2012/mar/08/political-empower-women-egypt (28 October 2012).

60. Lloyd-Roberts, "Has the Revolution Betrayed the Women of Egypt?" *BBC News* 13 February 2012, available at http://news.bbc.co.uk/2/hi/programmes/newsnight/9695850.stm (28 October 2012).

61. Ian Black, "Egypt bans Female Circumcision After Death of 12-year-old girl," *The Guardian* 29 June 2007, available at http://www.guardian.co.uk/world/2007/jun/30/gender.humanrights (28 October 2012).

62. Mariz Tadros, "Mutilating Bodies: The Muslim Brotherhood's Gift to Egyptian Women," *Open Democracy* 24 May 2012, available at http://www.opendemocracy.net/5050/mariz-tadros/mutilating-bodies-muslim-brotherhood%E2%80%99s-gift-to-egyptian-women (28 October 2012).

63. Jessica Gray, "Genital Mutilation: Islamist Parliamentarian Objects to Egypt's Ban on FGM," *WeNews* 28 March 2012, available at http://womensenews.org/story/genital-mutilation/120327/islamist-parliamentarian-objects-egypts-ban-fgm (28 October 2012).

64. Paul Schemm, "Morocco Elections: Islamist Party Wins," *The Huffington Post* 27 November 2011, available at http://www.huffingtonpost.com/2011/11/27/morocco-elections-islamist-party_n_1115425.html (28 October 2012).

65. Y.B. "Cheikh Maghraoui: Cet homme est dangereux," *Actuel* 25 May 2012, available at http://www.actuel.ma/Dossier/Cheikh_Maghraoui_Cet_homme_est_dangereux/1050.html (5 November 2012).

66. "Maroc: Une vedette transexuelle interdite à la television," *Demain Online* 12 April 2012, available at http://www.demainonline.com/2012/04/12/le-transsexuel-marocain-noor-interdit-de-tele/ (5 November 2012).

67. Ali Amar, ""Dix raisons de croire que le Maroc pourrait devenir un émirat islamiste," *Slate Afrique* 13 April 2012, available at http://www.slateafrique.com/85607/10-raisons-croire-que-le-maroc-pourrait-devenir-un-emirat-islamiste (5 November 2012).

68. Mohamed Saadouni, "Moroccan Women's Rights Groups Cry Foul," *Maghrebia* 12 July 2012, available at http://magharebia.com/en_GB/articles/awi/features/2012/07/12/feature-02 (5 November 2012).

69. "Morocco Sex Debate Rages After Imam's Death Call," *Al-Arabiya News* 8 July 2012, available at http://english.alarabiya.net/articles/2012/07/08/225161.html (5 November 2012).

70. Simon Martelli, "Sharia Law Declaration Raises Fears Among Women in New Libya," *Agence France-Presse* 24 October 2011, available at http://news.nationalpost.com/2011/10/24/sharia-law-declaration-raises-fears-among-women-in-new-libya/ (5 November 2012).

71. Quoted in Ansia Khaz Ali, "Iranian Women After the Islamic Revolution," *A Conflicts Forum Monograph* (July 2010), 4, available at http://conflictsforum.org/briefings/IranianWomenAfterIslamicRev.pdf (15 November 2012).

72. Alexander J. Zolan, "The Effect of Islamization on the Legal and Social Status of Women in Iran," *Boston College Third World Law Journal* 7, no. 2 (1987): 184.

73. Ibid., 185.

74. Ibid., 186.

75. Ibid., 188.

76. Talla Ralph, "Iran Bans Women from 77 University Degree Courses," *Global Post* 20 August 2012, available at http://www.globalpost.com/dispatch/news/regions/middle-east/iran/120820/iran-bans-women-university-degree-courses (15 November 2012).

77. Quoted in Janet Afary and Kevin B. Anderson, *Foucault and the Iranian Revolution: Gender and the Seductions of Islamism* (Chicago: University of Chicago Press, 2005), 99.

78. Quoted in David Zarnett, "Edward Said and the Iranian Revolution," *Democratiya* 9 (Summer 2007): 46, available at http://www.academia.edu/614917/Uncouth_nation_why_Europe_dislikes_America (15 November 2012).

79. Gert Van Langendonck, "Morocco: New magazine braves risks to give voice to Arab homosexuals," *Los Angeles Times* 28 April 2010, available at http://latimesblogs.latimes.com/babylonbeyond/2010/04/morocco-draft-new-magazine-gives-voice-to-arab-homosexuals-.html(15 November 2012).

80. Unfortunately, the online version of the magazine (www.mithly.net) no longer exists.

Conclusion

Focusing primarily on the western part of the Mediterranean, these pages have argued that many celebrated myths and apologies actually stand between Muslim women and significant reform. This book has endeavored to show that while Western imperialism and colonialism are often blamed for the status of Muslim women and men, reform-minded initiatives and agendas cannot hold the West solely responsible for Muslim women's precarious condition and status. Far more productive, from a feminist standpoint, would be an examination of myths propagated by Muslims and by non-Muslims alike in defense of religious symbols and institutions. For example, assuming that all the problems of Muslim women would be solved if only Muslims were to return to the "Golden Age," whether it is al-Andalus or another time, cannot help to achieve gender parity and equality. Ultimately, this book calls for a volitional and unconditional commitment to Muslim women's emancipation and gender justice, which cannot be achieved if reform is strictly confined within the boundaries of the sacred.

This commitment should come not just from Muslims; it should also be expected of those in the West who care about women, including those who have remained silent in the name of cultural relativism, or "tolerance" of others' values. In some instances, as discussed in chapters three and four, the call for "tolerance" has been interpreted as an invitation to bestow fantasies of liberation on symbols and practices that, from an objective and rational standpoint, are misogynist at best, inhumane and cruel at worst. Some feminists in the West may indeed choose to be "tolerant" of other cultures' sexist customs and violent practices, or they may find themselves obliged to be "understanding" lest they be accused of Islamophobia or of being agents of imperialism. But since when have feminists in the West been concerned with being "understanding" of patriarchal oppression of women? When it comes to issues related to their own bodies, liberties, and legal rights, feminists in the West have been anything but respectful of patriarchy and its institutions. They insisted that "the personal is political" and worked to challenge gender oppression as it affects them both as a group and as individuals everywhere including at home, at school, in the workplace, on the street, and in popular culture.

Now more than ever before, in our post-9/11 era and, even more recently, in the wake of the so-called Arab revolutions, there is an even greater need for Western feminist engagement, critique, theories, values, and tactics. The men's "Arab Spring" occurring in places such as Tunisia and Egypt is bringing regression rather than improvement in women's rights, as discussed in chapter 5. Moreover, the rise in anti-Western rhetoric predominant both in the Muslim world and among some liberals in the West has not worked to the advantage of Muslim women. At best, the anti-Western discourse has fueled existing skepticism toward feminism within Muslim countries. At worst, it has silenced unapologetic critique of misogynist practices, leaving Muslim women who dare to question religious laws and traditions vulnerable to ridicule, aggression, even death threats and *fatwas*. Unfortunately, these feminists do not receive much sympathy in the West because many scholars in the West are under the impression that feminism in the Muslim world has to justify itself within religion. Moreover, feminists who call for equality even if it is in conflict with the religious texts and traditions are assumed to represent only a minority. They are told that if the majority has voted for an Islamist government, then one should respect the election's outcome. But, since when has democracy been about supporting a majority at the expense of utterly crushing a minority? And more importantly, since when has feminism been in line with the views of the majority? Even if they were a minority in their communities and countries, still these women would deserve to be heard. Western secular feminists can provide them with solidarity and a platform from which they can be heard. In fact, Western feminists can at times be more effective in bringing about change faster given that, in addition to the West's long feminist tradition, Western feminists' right to cross boundaries, to criticize the sacred, and to rebel against conventions is protected by law, a privilege that many feminists in the Muslim world do not share. Western feminists therefore have a responsibility to these women in the Muslim world.

Calling for commitment from Western feminists, however, does not stem from a belief that Western feminism is without its problems. It goes without saying that feminism in the West did, and continues to, face numerous challenges. In fact, the succession of waves of feminism is in itself a reflection of and a response to such challenges. Nor does this book seek to institute a hierarchy by which the West is called upon to "save" the Muslim world. I do not advocate infantilizing or imposing "foreign" or Western values and ideas on Muslim societies. The point is to emphasize human rights, which, according to the Charter of the United Nations, are not exclusive to any particular gender or nation "large [or] small."[1] Hillary Rodham Clinton expressed it best in her remarks to the U.S. 4th World Conference on Women, delivered in Beijing, China, in 1995. She insisted that "It is a violation of human rights when women are doused with gasoline, set on fire, and burned to death," that "It is a violation of human rights when individual women are raped in their own communities," and that "It is a violation of human rights when a leading cause of death worldwide among women ages 14 to 44 is the violence they are subjected to in their own homes by their own relatives."[2] The violation of women's rights is not a separate category that can be dealt with later after all people are educated and have jobs, after a country achieves political stability, after a nation's economy reaches prosperity. The violation of women's rights is a violation of human rights, and as such, merits urgency.

Finally, the call for Western feminist commitment stems from the recognition of the shared humanity that unites women whether they are in New York, Casablanca, or Kandahar, and it is because of this shared humanity that it is okay for women of different cultures to meddle in each other's business. The Roman playwright of North African descent, Terrence, recognized this over two millennia ago. When, in one of his plays, *The Self Tormentor*, a character by the name of Chremes is told by his neighbor, a fellow farmer, to mind his own business, Chremes responded with the famous verse: *"Homo sum, humani nil a me alienum puto"* (I am human: nothing human is alien to me.)[3] Along the same lines, Western secular feminists have to stop being polite or politically correct, and instead start to meddle in other women's business, not because they are agents of imperialism, colonialism, or Orientalism. Rather, because they are human, and as such, nothing of the rape, suffering, and cruelty endured by Amina Filali, Fakhra Younus, and Najibia, the women whose stories introduce this book, is alien to them.

NOTES

1. The Charter of the United Nations can be accessed at http://www.un.org/en/documents/charter /preamble.shtml (15 August 2012).
2. Hillary Rodham Clinton, "Remarks to the United Nations Fourth World Conference on Women," Beijing, China 5 September 1995. The speech can be accessed at http://www.americanrhetoric.com/speeches /hillaryclintonbeijingspeech.htm (15 August 2012).
3. "The Self Tormentor," in *Terence*, trans. John Sargeant, Loeb Classical Library, vol. 1 (London: Heinemann, 1920), 77–78. In her discussion of cultural relativism, Elizabeth M. Zechenter also uses Terence's quote to make a case against cultural relativism. See Zechenter, "In the Name of Culture: Cultural Relativism and the Abuse of the Individual," *Journal of Anthropological Research*, 53, no 3 (Fall 1997): 319–47.

Selected Bibliography

Abdel-Karim, Gamal. "La evidencia islámica en la obra de Cervantes: análisis y valoración." 41–57 in *De Cervantes y el Islam*, ed. Nuria Martínez de Castilla Muñoz and Rodolfo Gil Benumeya Grimau. Madrid: Sociedad Estatal de Conmemoraciones Culturales, 2006.

Abu-Lughod, Janet L. *Before European Hegemony: The World System A.D. 1250–1350.* New York: Oxford University Press, 1989.

Abu-Lughod, Lila. "*Orientalism* and Middle East Feminist Studies," *Feminist Studies* 27, 1(2001): 101–13.

———. "Do Muslim Women Really Need Saving? Anthropological reflections on Cultural Relativism and Its Others." *American Anthropologist* 104 (2002): 783–90.

Adams, Susan M. et al. "The Genetic Legacy of Religious Diversity and Intolerance: Paternal Lineages of Christians, Jews, and Muslims in the Iberian Peninsula." *The American Journal of Human Genetics* 83 (December 2008): 725–736.

Afary, Janet and Kevin B. Anderson. *Foucault and the Iranian Revolution: Gender and the Seductions of Islamism.* Chicago: University of Chicago Press, 2005.

Ahmed, Leila. "Western Ethnocentrism and Perceptions of the Harem." *Feminist Studies* 8, no. 3 (1982): 521–34.

———. *Women and Gender in Islam: Historical Roots of a Modern Debate.* New Haven: Yale University Press, 1992.

———. *A Border Passage: From Cairo to America—A Woman's Journey.* New York: Farrar, Straus and Giroux, 1999.

Akhtar, Shabbir. *The Quran and the Secular Mind: A Philosophy of Islam.* New York: Routledge, 2008.

Al-Fassi, Hatoon Ajwad. *Women in Pre-Islamic Arabia: Nabataea.* Oxford: British Archaeological Reports International Series, 2007.

Al-Hazimi, Mansour, Ezzat Khattab, and Salma Khadra Jayyusi, ed. *Beyond the Dunes: An Anthology of Modern Saudi Literature.* New York: I.B. Tauris, 2006.

Ali, Tariq. *The Clash of Fundamentalisms: Crusades, Jihads and Modernity.* New York: Verso, 2002.

Allain, Jean. *International Law in the Middle East: Closer to Power than Justice.* Burlington: Ashgate, 2004.

Alloula, Malek. *The Colonial Harem*, trans. Myrna Godzich and Wlad Godzich. Minneapolis: University of Minnesota Press, 1986.

Appiah, Kwame Anthony. *In My Father's House: Africa in the Philosophy of Culture.* New York: Oxford University Press, 1992.

Aucassin et Nicolette and Other Tales, trans. Pauline Matarasso. Harmondsworth: Penguin, 1971.

Averroes (Ibn Rushd.) *Averroes on Plato's Republic.* Trans. Ralph Lerner. Ithaca: Cornell University Press, 1997.

Bargach, Jamila. *Orphans of Islam: Family, Abandonment, and Secret Adoption in Morocco.* New York: Rowman & Littlefield, 2002.

Barrett, Michele and Anne Phillips. "Introduction." 1–9 in *Destabilizing Theory: Contemporary Feminist Debates*, ed. Barrett and Phillips. Cambridge: Polity Press, 1992.

Bat Ye'or. *The Dhimmi: Jews and Christians under Islam.* Trans. David Maisel, Paul Fenton, and David Littman. Madison: Fairleigh Dickinson University Press, 1985.

Beau, Nicolas and Catherine Graciet. *La r égente de Carthage: maine basse sur la Tunisie.* Paris: Découverte, 2009.

Ben Jelloun, Tahar. *L'Enfant de sable*. Paris: Editions du Seuil, 1985.

Ben Chrouda, Lotfti and Isabelle Soares Boumalala. *Dans l'onbre de la reine par le major-dome des Ben Ali*. Paris: Michel Lafon, 2011.

Bin Laden, Osama. *Messages to the World: The Statements of Osama Bin Laden*. Ed. Bruce Lawrence. Trans. James Howarth. New York: Verso, 2005.

Board, Marilyn Lincoln. "Constructing Myths and Ideologies in Matisse's Odalisques." *Genders* 5(Summer 1989): 21–49.

Bordo, Susan. *Unbearable Weight: Feminism, Western Culture, and the Body*. Berkley: University of California Press, 1993.

Bouhdiba, Abdelwahab. *Sexuality in Islam*, trans. Alan Sheridan. London: Routledge Kegan Paul, 1985.

Brenon, Anne. "The Voice of the Good Women: An Essay on the Pastoral and Sacerdotal Role of Women in the Cathar Church." 114–33 in *Women Preachers and Prophets through Two Millennia of Christianity*, ed. Beverly Mayne Kienzle and Pamela J. Walker Berkeley: University of California Press, 1998.

Brownlee, Kevin. "Discourse as Proueces in *Aucassin et Nicolette*," *Yale French Studies* 70 (1986): 167–82.

Brustad, Kristen. *The Syntax of Spoken Arabic: A Comprehensive Study of Moroccan, Egyptian, Syrian, and Kuwaiti Dialects*. Washington: Georgetown University Press, 2000.

Bullock, Katherine. *Rethinking Muslim Women and the Veil: Challenging Historical and Modern Stereotypes*. Herndon: International Institute of Islamic Thought, 2002.

Burns, Jane. *Sea of Silk: A Textile Geography of Women's Work in Medieval French Literature*. Philadelphia: University of Pennsylvania Press, 2009.

Charrad, Mounira. *States and Women's Rights: The Making of Postcolonial Tunisia, Algeria, and Morocco*. Berkeley: University of California Press, 2001.

———. "From Nationalism to Feminism: Family Law in Tunisia." 111–136 in *Family in the Middle East: Ideational Change in Egypt, Iran and Tunisia*, ed. Kathryn Yount and Hoda Rashad. New York: Routledge, 2008.

Charrad, Mounira and Allyson Goeken. "Continuity or Change: Family Law and Family Structure in Tunisia." 27–47 in *African Families at the Turn of the 21st Century*, ed. Yaw Oheneba-Sakyi and Baffour K. Tayki. Westport: Praeger/Greenwood, 2006.

Chejne, Anwar. *Muslim Spain Its History and Culture*. Minneapolis: University of Minnesota Press, 1974.

Chilton, Bruce. *Abraham's Curse: Child Sacrifice in the Legacies of the West*. New York: Doubleday, 2008.

Claster, Jill N. *The Medieval Experience, 300–1400*. New York: New York University Press, 1982.

Coleman, Isobel. *Paradise Beneath Her Feet: How Women Are Transforming the Middle East*. New York: Random House, 2010.

Constable, Olivia Remie, ed. *Medieval Iberia: Readings from Christian, Muslim and Jewish Sources*. Philadelphia: University of Pennsylvania Press, 1997.

Constable, Olivia. *Trade and Traders in Muslim Spain*. Cambridge: Cambridge University Press, 1994.

Cook, David. *Martyrdom in Islam*. Cambridge: Cambridge University Press, 2007.

———. "The Muslim Man's Burden: Muslim Intellectuals Confront their Imperialist Past." 129– in *Postcolonial Theory and the Arab-Israeli Conflict*, ed. Donna Robinson Divine and Philip Carl Salzman. New York: Routledge, 2008.

Cooke, Miriam. *Women Claim Islam: Creating Islamic Feminism Through Literature*. New York: Routledge, 2001.

Dabashi, Hamid. *Brown Skin, White Masks*. London: Pluto Press, 2011.

———. *Post-Orientalism: Knowledge and Power in Time of Terror*. New Brunswick: Transaction Brooks, 2008.

Davis, Elizabeth Gould. *The First Sex*. New York: Putman, 1971.

Dean, Sharon L. *Constance Fenimore Woolson and Edith Wharton: Perspectives on Landscape and Art*. Knoxville: University of Tennessee Press, 2002.

DenBoer, James, ed. "String of Pearls: Sixty-Four 'Romance' *Kharjas* from Arabic and Hebrew *Muwashshahat* of the Eleventh-Thirteenth Centuries." *eHumanista* (Monographs in Humanities, 6). Web. September 2011. http://www.ucsb.edu/projects/ehumanista/projects.

Djebar, Assia. *Vaste est la prison*. Paris: Albin Michel, 1995.

Eller, Cynthia. *The Myth of Matriarchal Prehistory: Why an Invented Past Won't Give Women a Future*. Boston: Beacon, 2000.

Flesler, Daniela. *The Return of the Moor: Spanish Responses to Contemporary Moroccan Immigration*. West Lafayette: Purdue University Press, 2008.

Foster, David William, ed. *Spanish Writers on Gay and Lesbian Themes: A bio-critical sourcebook*. Westport: Greenwood Press, 1999.

Foucault, Michel. *The Archaeology of Knowledge and the Discourse on Language*, trans. A. M. S. Smith. New York: Pantheon Books, 1972.

———. *Discipline and Punish: The Birth of the Prison*, trans. Alan Sheridan. New York: Pantheon Books, 1977.

Fuchs, Barbara. *Exotic Nation: Maurophilia and the Construction of Early Modern Spain*. Philadelphia: University of Philadelphia Press, 2009.

Garcés, María Antonia. *Cervantes in Algiers: A Captive's Tale*. Nashville: Vanderbilt University Press, 2002.

Gerecht, Reuel Marc. *The Wave: Man, God, and the Ballot Box in the Middle East*. Stanford: Hoover Institution Press Publication, 2011.

Ghoussoub, Mai. "Feminist—or the Eternal Masculine—in the Arab World." *New Left Review* 161 (January–February 1987): 3–18.

Gill, John. *Andalucía: A Cultural History*. New York: Oxford University Press, 2009.

Griffin, Robert. "*Aucassin et Nicolette* and the Albigensian Crusade," *Modern Language Quarterly* 26 (1965): 243–56.

Habib, Samar. *Female Homosexuality in the Middle East: Histories and Representations*. New York: Routledge, 2009.

Hamilton, Michelle. *Representing Others in Medieval Iberian Literature*. New York: Palgrave, 2007.

Hasyim, Syafiq. *Understanding Women in Islam: An Indonesian Perspective*. Jakarta: Solstice, 2006.

Heath, Jeffrey. *Jewish and Muslim Dialects of Moroccan Arabic*. New York: Routledge, 2002.

Hernández Cruz, Victor. *In the Shadow of al-Andalus: Poems*. Minneapolis: Coffee House Press, 2011.

Homza, Lu Ann, ed. *The Spanish Inquisition, 1478–1614: An Anthology of Sources*. Indianapolis: Hackett, 2006.

Hoodfar, Homa. "The Veil in Their Minds and on Our Heads: Veiling Practices and Muslim Women." 248–79 in *The Politics of Culture in the Shadow of Capital*, ed. Lisa Lowe and David Lloyd. Durham: Duke University Press, 1997.

Hussain, Jamila. *Islam, Its Law and Society*. Sydney: Federation Press, 2003.

Ibn Hazm. *The Ring of the Dove: A Treatise on the Art and Practice of Arab Love*, trans. A. J. Arberry. London: Luzac, 1953.

Ibn Warraq. *Defending the West: A Critique of Edward Said's Orientalism*. Amherst: Prometheus Books, 2007.

Jayyusi, Salma Khadra. "Andalusi Poetry: The Golden Period." 317–66 in *The Legacy of Muslim Spain*. Ed. Salma Khadra Jayyusi. Leiden: Brill, 1992.

Johnson, Carroll B. "Phantom Pre-texts and Fictional Authors: Sidi Hamid Benengeli, *Don Quijote* and the Metafictional Conventions of Chivalric Romances." *Cervantes Bulletin of the Cervantes Society of America* 27.1(2007): 179–99.

Kabbani, Rana. *Europe's Myths of Orient*. London: McMillan, 1986.

Kahf, Mohja. *Western Representations of the Muslim Woman: From Termagant to Odalisque*. Austin: University of Texas Press, 1999.

Karam, Azza. *Women, Islamists and the State: Contemporary Feminists in Egypt*. London: Macmillan Press, 1998.

Khaz Ali, Ansia. "Iranian Women After the Islamic Revolution," *A Conflicts Forum Monograph* (July 2010): 1–21.

Kennedy, Valerie. *Edward Said: A Critical Introduction*. Cambridge: Polity Press, 2000.

Kundera, Milan. *The Book of Laughter and Forgetting*. Trans. Michael Henry Heim. New York: Penguin, 1981.

Fakhry, Majid. *The Quran: A Modern English Version*. Reading: Garnet, 1997.

Lampert-Weissig, Lisa. *Medieval Literature and Postcolonial Studies*. Edinburgh: Edinburgh University Press, 2010.

Lazreg, Marnia. *The Eloquence of Silence*. New York: Routledge, 1994.

———. "Feminism and Difference: The Perils of Writing as a Woman on Women in Algeria." 326–48 in *Conflicts in Feminism*, ed. Marianne Hirsche and Evelyn Fox Keller. New York: Routledge, 1990.

———. *Questioning the Veil: Open Letters to Muslim Women*. Princeton: Princeton University Press, 2009.

Lebbadi, Hasna. *Feminist Traditions in Andalusi-Moroccan Oral Narratives*. New York: Palgrave, 2009.

———. "Fatima Mernissi's *Dreams of Trespass*: Self Representation or Confinement within the Discourse of Otherness." 129–39 in *North-South Linkages and Connections in Continental and Diaspora African Literatures*, ed. Edris Makward, Mark Lilleleht, and Ahmed Saber. Trenton: Africa World Press, 2005.

Lee, Hermione. *Edith Wharton*. London: Vintage, 2007.

Lewis, Bernard, ed. *A Middle East Mosaic: Fragments of Life, Letters, and History*. New York: Random, 2000.

Lewis, Reina. *Gendering Orientalism: Race, Femininity and Representation*. London: Routledge, 1996.

Liu, Benjamin M. and James T. Monroe. *Ten Hispano-Arabic Strophic Songs in the Modern Oral Tradition Music and Texts*. University of California Publications in Modern Philology, 125. Berkeley: University of California Press, 1989.

López-Baralt, Luce. *Islam in Spanish literature: from the Middle Ages to the present*. Trans. Andrew Hurley. Leiden: Brill, 1992.

López de la Plaza, Gloria. *Al-Andalus: Mujeres, Sociedad y Religión*. Malaga: University of Malaga, 1992.

Majid, Anouar. "The Politics of Islamic Feminism," *Signs: Journal of Women and Culture in Society* 23.1(1998): 321–61.

Manji, Irshad. *The Trouble with Islam: A Muslim's Call for Reform in Her Faith*. New York: St. Martin's Press, 2004.

Marín, Manuela. "Marriage and Sexuality in al-Andalus." In *Marriage and Sexuality in Medieval and Early Modern Iberia*. Ed. Eukene Lacarra Lanz. New York: Routledge, 2002.

Massad, Joseph A. *Desiring Arabs*. Chicago: University of Chicago Press, 2006.

Melman, Billie. *Women's Orients: English Women and the Middle East, 1718–1918: Sexuality, Religion and Work*. Ann Arbor: University of Michigan Press, 1996.

Menocal, Maria Rosa. *The Ornament of the World: How Muslims, Jews, and Christians Created a Culture of Tolerance in Medieval Spain*, New York: Little Brown, 2002.

Mernissi, Fatima. *Beyond the Veil: Male Female Dynamics in Muslim Society*. London: Al Saqi Books, 1985.

———. *Islam and Democracy: Fear of the Modern World*, trans. Mary Jo Lakeland. Reading: Addison-Wesley, 1991.

———. *Dreams of Trespass: Tales of a Harem Girlhood*. Reading: Addison-Wesley, 1994.

———. *The Veil and the Male Elite: A Feminist Interpretation of Women's Rights in Islam*, trans. Mary Jo Lakeland. Reading: Addison-Wesley, 1991.

———. *The Forgotten Queens of Islam*. Trans. Mary Jo Lakeland. Minneapolis: University of Minnesota Press, 1993.

———. *Scheherazade Goes West: Different Cultures, Different Harems*. New York: Washington Square Press, 2001.

Meyer, Leisa D. Creating *G.I. Jane: Sexuality and Power in the Women's Army Corps during World War II*. New York: Columbia University Press, 1996.

Mirrer, Louise. *Women, Jews, and Muslims in the Texts of Reconquest Castile*. Ann Arbor: University of Michigan Press, 1996.

Moghissi, Haideh. *Feminism and Islamic Fundamentalism: The Limits of Posmodern Analysis*. London: Zed Books, 1999. 17.

Monroe, James. "A Curious Morisco Appeal to the Ottoman Empire." *Al-Andalus* 31(1966): 281–303.

Montaner, Carlos Alberto. *Twisted Roots: Latin America's Living Past*. New York: Algora, 2003.

Montávez, Pedro Martínez. *Al-Andalus, España, en la literature árabe contemporánea: La casa del pasado*. Madrid: MAPFRE, 1992.

"Morocco Sex Debate Rages After Imam's Death Call." *Al-Arabiya News*. 8 July 2012. Available at http://english.alarabiya.net/articles/2012/07/08/225161.html

Al-Nafzaoui, Muhammad ibn Muhammad [Cheikh Nefzaoui]. *The Perfumed Garden of the Cheikh Nefzaoui: A Manual of Arabian Erotology*. Trans. Sir Richard F. Burton. New York: Signet Classics, 1999.

Nochlin, Linda. "The Imaginary Orient." *Art in America*, (May 1983): 118–131; 187–191.

Nykl, Alois R. *Hispano-Arabic Poetry and Its Relations with the Old Provençal Troubadours*. Baltimore: J.H. Furst, 1946.

Orvietani Busch, Silvia. *Medieval Mediterranean Ports: The Catalan and Tuscan Coasts, 1100 to 1235*. Leiden: Brill, 2001.

Prado-Vilar, Francisco. "The Gothic Anamorphic Gaze: Regarding the Worth of Others." 67–100 in *Under the Influence: Questioning the Comparative in Medieval Castile*. Leiden: Brill, 2005.

Ramey, Lynn Tarte. *Christian, Saracen and Genre in Medieval French Literature*. New York: Routledge, 2001.

Rhouni, Raja. *Secular and Islamic Feminist Critiques in the Work of Fatima Mernissi*. Leiden: Brill, 2010.

Ricoeur, Paul. *On Translation*. Trans. Eileen Brennan. New York: Routledge, 2006.

Ringrose, David. *Spain, Europe, and the "Spanish miracle", 1700–1900*. Cambridge: Cambridge University Press, 1996.

Robinson, Cynthia. *Medieval Andalusian Courtly Culture in the Mediterranean: Hadith Bayad wa Riyad*. New York: Routledge, 2007.

Roth, Benita. *Separate Roads to Feminism: Black, Chicana, and White Feminist Movements in America's Second Wave*. New York: Cambridge University Press, 2004.

Roth, Norman. *Jews, Visigoths and Muslims in Medieval Spain: Cooperation and Conflict*. Leiden: Brill, 1994.

Routledge, Michael. "Songs." 91–111 in *The Oxford Illustrated History of the Crusades*, ed. Jonathan Riley-Smith. Oxford: Oxford University Press, 1997.

Rubiera Mata, Maria Jesus, ed. *Poesia femenina hispano-arabe*. Madrid: Castalia, 1989.

Sadiqi, Amina. *Women, Gender, and Language in Morocco*. Leiden: Brill, 2003.

Said, Edward. *Orientalism*. New York: Vintage Books, 1979.

Schaefer-Rodríguez, Claudia. *Juan Goytisolo: del 'realismo crítico' a la utopia*. Madrid: Porrúa Turranzas, 1984.

Scheper-Hughes, Nancy and Philip Bourgois eds. *Violence in War and Peace: An Anthology*. Malden: Blackwell University Press, 2004.

Shahidian, Hammed. *Women in Iran: Emerging Voices in the Women's Movement*. Westport: Greenwood Press, 2002.

Sensibar, Judith L. "Edith Wharton as Propagandist and Novelist." 149–71 in *A Forward Glance: New Essays on Edith Wharton*, ed. Clare Cloquitt, Susan Goodman, and Candace Waid. Newark: University of Delaware Press, 1999.

Shahar, Shulamith. *Women in a Medieval Heretical Sect: Agnes and Huguette the Waldensians*, trans. Yael Lotan. Woodbridge: Boydell Press, 2001.

Shryock, Andrew. *Islamophobia/Islamophilia: Beyond the Politics of Enemy and Friend*. Bloomington: Indiana University Press, 2010.

Song of Roland, The. Trans. Glyn Burgess. London: Penguin, 1990.

Songs of Holy Mary of Alfonso X, The Wise: A Traslation of the Cantigas de Santa Maria, trans. Kathleen Kulp-Hill. Tempe: Arizona Center for Medieval and Renaissance Studies, 2000.

Spivak, Gayatri Chakravorty. *A Critique of Postcolonial Reason: Toward a History of the Vanishing Present.* Cambridge: Harvard University Press, 1999.

Steinem, Gloria. *Wonder Woman.* New York: Reinhart and Winston, 1972.

Stewart, Devin J. "Ibn Zaydun." In *Cambridge History of Arabic Literature: The Literature of al-Andalus.* Ed. Maria Rosa Menocal and Michael Sells. Cambridge: Cambridge UP, 2000. 306–16.

Stone, Gregory. *Dante's Pluralism and the Islamic Philosophy of Religion.* New York: Palgrave Macmillan, 2006.

Taylor, Diana. *Disappearing Acts: Spectacles of Gender and Nationalism in Argentina's Dirty War.* Durham: Duke University Press, 1997.

Terence. "The Self Tormentor," in *Terence,* trans. John Sargeant, Loeb Classical Library, vol. 1. London: Heinemann, 1920.

Al-Tifashi, Ahmad. *The Delight of Hearts, or What You will Not Find in Any Book.* San Francisco: Gay Sunshine Press, 1988.

Tolan, John Victor. *Saracens: Islam in the Medieval European Imagination.* New York: Columbia University Press, 2002.

Ugarte, Michael. "Juan Goytisolo: Unruly Disciple of Américo Castro." *Journal of Spanish Studies: Twentieth Century,* 7 (1979): 353–64.

Van den Broek, Roel of. "The Cathars: Medieval Gnostics?" 78–108 in *Gnosis and Hermeticism: From Antiquity to Modern Times,* ed. Roel of van den Broek and Wouter J. Hanegraaff (New York: SUNY Press, 1998), 89.

Viguera Molíns, María Jesús. "A Borrowed Space: Andalusi and Maghribi Women in Chronicles." In *Writing the Feminine: Women in Arab Sources.* Eds. Manuela Marín and Randi Deguilhem. New York: I.B. Tauris, 2002. 165–180.

Wadud, Amina. *Inside the Gender Jihad: Women's Reform in Islam.* Oxford: Oneworld, 2006.

Weber, Charlotte. "Unveiling Scheherazade: Feminist Orientalism in the International Alliance of Women, 1911–1950," *Feminist Studies,* 27.1 (2001): 125–57.

Weever, Jacqueline de. *Sheba's Daughters: Whitening and Demonizing the Saracen Woman in Medieval French Epic.* New York: Garland, 1998.

Wharton, Edith. *In Morocco.* New York: Charles Scribner's Sons, 1920. Reprint. Hopewell: Ecco Press, 1996.

Wistrich, Robert S. *Muslim Anti-Semitism: A Clear and Present Danger.* New York: American Jewish Committee, 2002.

Wolf, Naomi. *The Beauty Myth: How Images of Beauty Are Used Against Women.* New York: Doubleday, 1991.

Woodhull, Winifred. *Transfigurations o the Maghreb: Feminism, Decolonization, and Literatures.* Minneapolis: University of Minnesota Press, 1993.

Yegenoglu, Meyda. *Colonial Fantasies: Towards a Feminist Reading of Orientalism* Cambridge: Cambridge University Press, 1998.

Zarnett, David. "Edward Said and the Iranian Revolution." *Democratiya* 9 (Summer 2007): 43–53.

Zechenter, Elizabeth M. "In the Name of Culture: Cultural Relativism and the Abuse of the Individual." *Journal of Anthropological Research,* 53, no 3 (Fall 1997): 319–47.

Zeiger, Susan. *In Uncle Sam's Service: Women Workers with the American Expeditionary Force.* Ithaca: Cornell University Press, 2000.

Zolan, Alexander J. "The Effect of Islamization on the Legal and Social Status of Women in Iran," *Boston College Third World Law Journal* 7, no. 2 (1987): 183–93.

Zwartjes, Otto. *Love Songs from Al-Andalus: History, Structure and Meaning of the Kharja.*

Index

About the Author

Ibtissam Bouachrine was born and raised in Casablanca, Morocco. After graduating *summa cum laude* and Phi Beta Kappa from West Virginia University, she attended Florida State University and earned a Ph.D. in medieval Iberian literatures and cultures at Tulane University. She is associate professor in the Department of Spanish and Portuguese and the Director of Middle East Studies at Smith College. While her research is centered on questions of gender and sexuality in Islam, she has also published on feminism and democracy in North Africa, Islam in Europe, and Muslim-Western relations before and since 1492.